They Rejected the Chief Cornerstone

Author: William Pittenger

TABLE OF CONTENTS

APPENDICES

CHAPTER ONE
SOVEREIGNTY VERSES INTERNATIONAL LAW

National Security

National security is extremely important. It allows our military troops to be trained in times of peace. It fosters the growth of companies that manufacture and provide important services to the general public. Trade secrets are kept within the walls of the business to pass down to future generations. Family traditions such as; farming, fishing, food services, carpentry, automobiles, and clothing manufacturing, are handed down as a way of protecting our way of life. National security allows peaceful families to work and make a living within the borders of a nation without fear of attack from foreign powers. In order to facilitate peace and aid in enforcing law and order, soldiers are commissioned to guard our nation to protect our ideals as outlined in the Constitution of the United States. It is also why we should have operational oil rigs built in the coastal areas of the United States, because there will be security on and around the rigs. Businesses have the right to protect themselves from theft and vandalism, and the crews of the rigs and security teams would report any activity that would harm the security of the nation.

Border Protection

In every nation, there is a need for border protection. North and South Korea are separated by the Demilitarized Zone (DMZ), a false border created by a stalemate and a peace treaty. It is protected on both the north side and the south side. There are guard towers with armed men and units rotate their soldiers to and from those towers twenty-four hours a day and seven days a week. Other nations aid the United States in protecting

South Korea from an invasion from North Korea. Through great coordination and a show of force, the border remains intact, while those who are found in the mile-wide DMZ without authorization are shot. Troops are stationed on the coastlines, and on the southern island, where the Republic of Korea (ROK) Special Forces units train. The government of South Korea and its people chose to live in a capitalist society under a democracy with freedom to choose their paths of life. The only things different in South Korea are the language and that all males must serve in the ROK army for three years prior to getting a job and marrying. People understand that in order to maintain their way of life, that there must be a strong military presence to defend against attack from inferior nations. The United States has partnered with South Korea by providing a skeleton force of soldiers that aid in the training of Korean Augmentations to the United States Army (KATUSA).

The United States government believes that it is important to aid partner nations in developing a strong capitalist economy, democracy, and a strong self-defense. If it is important to the United States in providing border protection and patrol to other nations, it should be pretty clear that there should be active duty military units along our nation's borders and coastal areas to provide for national defense against enemies that attempt to invade.

The United States Constitution

In Article I, Section 8 of the Constitution, it says,

"The Congress shall have Power To lay and collect Taxes, Duties, Imposts, and excises, to pay the Debts and provide for the common Defence and general Welfare of the United States; but all Duties, Imposts, and Excises shall be uniform throughout the United States, . . ."

"To constitute Tribunals inferior to the supreme Court; . . ."

"To declare War, grant Letters of Marque and Reprisal, and make Rules concerning Captures on Land and Water;"

4

"To raise and support Armies, but no Appropriation of Money to that Use shall be for a term longer than two Years; . . ."

"To provide for calling forth the Militia to execute the Laws of the Union, suppress Insurrections and repel Invasions;

"To provide for organizing, arming, and disciplining, the Militia, and for governing such Part of them as may be employed in the Service of the United States, reserving to the States respectively, the Appointment of the Officers, and the Authority of training the Militia according to the discipline prescribed by Congress; . . ."

According to the Constitution, it's clear that Congress is responsible for the training and payment of troops for the purposes of maintaining federal law and order, frustrate and disband rebellious groups, and defeat invading armies. States have the right to appoint officers, and have the authority of Congress to train the armies in the manner prescribed by Congress.

In Article I, Section 10, it says,

"No State shall, without the Consent of congress, lay any Duty of Tonnage, keep Troops, or Ships of War in time of Peace, enter into any Agreement or Compact with another State, or with a foreign Power, or engage in War, unless actually invaded, or in such imminent Danger as will not admit of delay."

Article IV, Section 4 states:

"The United States shall guarantee to every State in this Union a Republican Form of Government, and shall protect each of them against Invasion; and on Application of the Legislature, or of the Executive (when the Legislature cannot be convened), against domestic Violence."

Written in black and white, individual states are forbidden to engage in war, unless they are invaded and the state cannot wait on the federal government to take action. It cannot be misinterpreted. There can be no spin. It wasn't a mistake.

According to the Constitution, Arizona has been invaded by illegal immigrants passing through Mexico's border. They are shipping drugs, humans, and murdering people in cold blood as they come across. Those that choose to settle in Arizona without being documented, are costing billions of dollars of state tax money to support their children, medical needs, and education. The state of Arizona declared an emergency to pass a bill that would give the police the permission to insure illegal immigrants (specifically related to crimes) are detained, processed, and deported (AZ SB 1070, Article 8, Section 11-1051, Sub-sections A-J; referencing US Code Article 8 Section 1229 a and c, 1304e, and 1306a). This was because Congress ignored the many pleas of the Arizona legislature to Congress and the White House to close the border and provide active duty troops to the southern border states.

Given the fact that the entire Southwest is populated by nearly 50% Latinos, and over half of those are here illegally, it simply doesn't make sense that other states have not done the same. The United States is under attack by alien insurgents coming across the Mexican border, and the citizens of Arizona are under imminent danger. If, then, Arizona is in imminent danger, then it's pretty clear to me that Texas, California, New Mexico, Nevada, and Colorado are too. Therefore, according to the Constitution, Congress is required by the Law of the Land to suppress and repel them. This law has nothing to do with legal and naturalized citizens of the United States. It has nothing to do with race, color, creed, or religion. Illegal aliens, in general, are simply breaking the law, and they cannot get away with it.

Since the federal government doesn't see the urgency of the situation, and has taken nearly fifty years to anything about it, then the states, if they so desire, have the permission to take action on their own until Congress does something about it.

The problem with individual states taking care of it is that laws cannot supersede the Constitution. Some governors or state legislative bodies may go too far in creating laws that are unConstitutional. Legislators have to be careful to insure they are not overstepping the Law of the Land to obtain peace until the federal government can step in with the necessary armies.

This isn't a job for civilian border patrol or the National Guard. It's a job for the United States four military forces. Our soldiers gave their lives in World War I, II, the Korean War, Viet Nam, Bosnia, Iraq, and

Afghanistan. Isn't it about time they fought for their OWN country?

CHAPTER TWO
RULE OF LAW

Moral, Just, and Humane

The Constitution, with the Declaration of Independence is a positive document. Very little of these documents refer to negative consequences. These documents spell out the God-given rights of mankind in general, then specifically, Americans. So, in determining what applies to American citizens, it can be determined what doesn't apply to non-citizens. Citizens (even government officials) may practice the religion of their choice, exercise freedom of speech, the press, may assemble peaceably, and petition the Government for a redress of grievances (US Constitution, Amendment I).

People have the right to privacy. That means that anything on their person, anything they have with them, anything on their property, and in their houses cannot be confiscated or searched without a warrant or probable cause. If a warrant is issued, it must be by a proper authority (a judge), requested by those who enforce the law upon suspicion based on actions, exchanges, conversation, violence, or witnesses attesting to them. Moreover, it must specify people, places, and things to be searched or confiscated, and the reason why (Amendment IV).

No one can be held for a crime without an indictment of a Grand Jury, or be convicted of the same crime after being tried and found innocent. No one can be forced to testify against himself, and he cannot be deprived of life, liberty, or property without due process of law (Amendment V). Additionally, the use of imminent domain of private property without payment is illegal.

An accused has the right to be informed, a speedy and public trial before an impartial jury within the district of the crime, have legal counsel, and the right to obtain witnesses in his defense, and to be confronted by his accusers (Amendment VI).

Excessive bail, fines, nor cruel and unusual punishments may not be imposed (Amendment VIII).

Power, position, and wealth do not assign people more rights than others, nor are the rights of others denied them in the absence of power, position, and wealth (Amendment IX).

The people of the individual states have jurisdiction in their states when the federal government does not (Amendment X). In other words, our form of government is decentralized. The federal government doesn't impose itself on the states, and the states may create laws that complement the Constitution without superceding it. States cannot make laws in opposition to the Constitution, or the federal government has the right to force state governments to comply with the federal law, as in the case of a black student in Arkansas who was escorted to school and protected by the United States Army. The state governor refused to comply with the Constitutional requirement to desegregate schools.

Officials of the federal government cannot be sued by its citizens, nor can it be sued by foreign powers (Amendment XI). A foreign power would be, for instance, England, Russia, Spain, France, Saudi Arabia, Iran, Iraq, Mexico, Canada, Israel, or any other non-US nation, even if it is a part of the United Nations (I don't mean to sound sarcastic, but I thought I might define "foreign powers." It seems people have forgotten). Allowing the UN to make the United States within its jurisdiction is unConstitutional. It cannot impose laws upon the federal government or sue the United States. We have to abide by the laws of the countries we visit, and others have to abide by our laws when they visit. However, countries make their own laws and enforce their own laws. We must govern ourselves. We may contribute to the UN, but we do not answer to the UN. It's a partnership of nations based upon international commerce, and mutual respect. That's as far as it should go.

People who are the age of 18 and law abiding citizens of all colors, religions, creeds, education, or sex may vote regardless of employment. Law abiding citizens have not been party to insurrections against the United States, nor have partnered with the enemy during times of war (Amendments XIV - section 2; XV - section 1; and XIX). Illegal aliens are breaking the law by being here. So, they don't have any rights, nor can they vote. Mexicans that are here illegally are acting as insurgents against the United States. So again, they don't have any rights and can't vote. They don't even have the right to a redress of grievances, which means that they don't have the legal right to demonstrate. They're not citizens. They're not Americans. They aren't under the jurisdiction of laws of the United States. They are under the jurisdiction of the Mexican government. Family or not, aiding and abetting criminals is a crime. It's the Law of the Land.

The document is a positive document, and outlines the rights of citizens by birth or naturalization living by the laws. Merely being born in the United States is not enough.

Over-crowding of Jails

A dangerous trend has developed over the years. It almost seems as if figures in the world of crime have been plotting to over-run the United States by repetitively breaking the law and filling up the jails. Crimes seem to be petty in nature. Their punishments are relatively small for a first-offender. Stack these petty crimes up, and a repeat offender can end up with a sentence of ten or more years. Murderers, grand theft criminals, and those who commit crimes on a mass scale can be imprisoned for life without parole. Those who are on death row may not be put to death for years after they have been sentenced. I believe that the waiting period should only be six months between conviction and death, to allow for ONE appeal with sufficient evidence to acquit the detained. After six months, however, the execution must take place. It frees up space and saves taxpayers money. I hope they get saved, and may God have mercy in the after-life.

Due to the appeal process, many dangerous criminals may be set free who were not rehabilitated as a result of their sentencing. This allows them to continue in the same behaviors that put them in jail, to begin with, and they inevitably end up right back in jail. Some who have been let out of prison have no idea, outside a life of crime, how to live as free individuals, so for no other reason than having a roof over their heads and three meals a day, they end up back in jail.

The effect that this has on society is that these criminals, upon their release, cause a great deal of fear. Law abiding people who were targets know that prison, in most cases, does not rehabilitate a criminal, and may come back. Sometimes, it happens, and the victim has to endure not only another violation of rights, but may face death. There are many stories in the news all over the world about it. Yet, it continues in a vicious cycle.

Rampant crime committed by both repeat offenders and hardened criminals causes jails to be full beyond capacity. Since wardens cannot legally over-crowd people within their walls, people who regularly break the law are generally kept in jail for perhaps a week or two, then let them go with a fine or probation. Sentencing cannot be properly carried out, and people don't pay for their crimes. They have no regard for the law because there are no real consequences for their actions.

The death penalty is for those who, by an act of their own will with full and conscious choices, commit heinous crimes, such as murder in cold blood, mass murder, or violent sex offences. People who commit such crimes have crossed the line of Moral Conscience. Once the line has been crossed, there is no turning back. The death penalty is imposed as a punishment for the behavior, and is an act of mercy to the general public, alleviating the fear that the person will kill again when released.

The laws concerning murder in Old Testament Israel in approximately 1451 BC state that those who killed out of hatred and jealousy, and killed indiscriminately someone that was not an enemy, polluted the land. Therefore, they should either be put to death, or flee to one of the six cities of refuge until the anointed high priest died. The cities were more or less prisons. Bounty hunters were paid to find the murderers, and could not enter these cities. If the murderer was found outside the borders, the bounty hunter could kill the murderer without penalty (Numbers 35:15-28). I'm not advocating that we should allow members of the clergy to convict men and women of crimes, but in the days before Christ, priests were well educated in not only religious matters, but in political matters and the law. They were to live pure lives from the inside out, because they were the representatives of God to the people and taught kings how to rule. They weren't perfect people, but when they sinned, they had to insure that they obeyed the law concerning purity from sin and repentance. They offered a sacrifice like everyone else, and then continued in their offices of priests. This was critical, because priests offered sacrifices to God on the altar of the Ark of the Covenant in the Holy of Holies. If a high priest was not pure in heart upon entrance to the Holy of Holies, God would strike the sin, killing the man, and the sins of the people would not be covered that year (http://www.shalomnyc.org/feasts/yom_kippur.htm).

The death penalty also instills a healthy respect for the laws, and a healthy fear of breaking them. When children are taught that there are bad consequences for bad decisions (even death), there will be less crime, jails will not be over-crowded, and society will not be overtaken by criminals who have no regard for the law or human life.

CHAPTER THREE
MAJORITY RULES

Wealth does not equal a majority

In the United States, our forefathers wanted to fundamentally change the way governments interacted with people and how people were governed. According to W. Cleon Skousen, National Center for Constitutional Studies, a democracy works for small populations, but becomes less of a form of representation as the population grows (The 5,000 Year Leap, c. 2009; p. 154). A democracy is when a group of 20 meets, discusses, and votes on decisions. Inevitably, that group of 20 becomes 200, and they will meet, discuss, and vote on discussions. Information becomes watered down, some of it doesn't reach the people, some people forget the meetings or can't meet, or only a few meet and make the decisions. Now, imagine 10 groups of 20. As the population grows to 2000, there may only be 20 people meeting. Twenty people may or may not make decisions based on what is best for the people at large. Those 20 people may even meet without the rest of the population knowing. It then creeps back into the same forms of government that our forefathers were attempting to evade; totalitarianism, elitism, and eventually socialism. Socialism is rule by convenience. It's a master management plan designed to categorize people into specific groups, or classes. These classes become the root of a caste system. A caste system locks people, their families, and their successors into sects. This creates hierarchies of poverty, middle class, and upper class citizens in which there is no promotion, and a population is segregated. Like ranks in the military, fraternization from one class to another (except for employer to employee, in that order), is discouraged and looked down upon.

The form of government our forefathers created was one step beyond a democracy. They created a republic, in which there would be a proportionate amount of representatives assigned to any given population, called districts. Representatives have the responsibility of remaining in contact with their constituents, and speak on behalf of the majority in those districts. Texas would have more representation than Oklahoma. The populations differ. The result would be a more accurate description of the representation of the majority as the elected officials voiced the opinions of the people in their districts. A republic, if used properly, would then frustrate any single class of people from dictating law or imposing taxes without their express consent. What would be, in a caste system, segregated populations, a republic allows for these groups to be intertwined and free to rise and fall, and rise again.

Therefore, a more equal representation of the differing classes of people over the age of 18 in a district, whether poor or wealthy, educated or uneducated, regardless of vocation, race, color, creed, or religion would be the result. The Constitution made it clear that criminals or those that had participated in rebellion, had no representation. Depending on the proportion of criminals (those in jail) to the moral population, a district with the same population as another may have less elected officials to voice their opinion (Amendment XIV, Section 2).

Legal arguments vs. the Constitution

The reason that the self-governing Republic of the United States was created by our forefathers was to give the masses the power to prevent special interest and elite groups that think they "know better" from pushing ruses of unwanted legislation and false agendas on them without consent. Self-governing countries are populated by educated people who refuse to be lied to, manipulated, or mistreated. Though elected representatives were to voice the opinions of the American people, we are not to entirely trust that they will do what they are supposed to do (Skousen; pp. 163-164). It is our responsibility to make our voices known through phone calls, letters, and occasionally a detailed study to present our views. Silence is assumed to be approval. It is our responsibility to remain educated about the Constitution, the laws, the history that brought us here, our rights as Americans, and to fight for the way of life that our forefathers created for us. There is no other America!

We need to be educated so that no one can blind us with smooth talk. We need to know the Constitution because it is the dispensational document that gives us our rights. We need to know the laws so that we don't break them. We need to remind others and teach our children to respect them. We need to know history so that we can be reminded of successes and failures so that we can fail less and succeed more. We need to stand ready to fight against those who want to take our heritage away from us. Our forefathers knew that common people weren't lawyers, so they created a document that a child could understand. The Constitution is not written in Latin. It applies to the wealthy land owner in a mansion as well as the law-abiding poor man living in a box in the alley, as long as they are natural born or naturalized citizens of the United States.

The Constitution, even in a 2″ x 3″ pamphlet is 36 pages with the Declaration of Independence. The thesis is "...life, liberty, and the pursuit of happiness (The Declaration of Independence. July 4th, 1776). The problem with legal arguments is that they tend to get lengthy. The health care bill was over 2000 pages long. When the health care bill passed, Senator Nancy Pelosi said, "I'm glad the health care bill passed so that we can find out what's in it!" It was long, had earmarks (last minute unreviewed additions), and contained unconstitutional provisions in it. I smell another rat! Who's writing the laws if Congress has no idea what was written?

CHAPTER FOUR
CAPITALISM VS. COMMUNISM

Capitalism: The Market Driven Economy

Capitalism and free market principals go hand-in-hand. When people are free to choose their vocations, they become educated so that they are good at what they do. When people provide a product or service by free will, they will be excellent providers above others. The drive behind excellence in America is "...life, liberty, and the pursuit of happiness," at its fullest. Capitalism is a monetary structure that is designed to allow a free people to prosper under fair laws. Since capitalism is based upon freedom, then people may freely conduct their affairs of commerce without a government entity looking over their shoulders.

According to Adam Smith, in a book called "An Inquiry into the Nature and Causes of the Wealth of Nations," written in 1776, the economy is governed by an "invisible hand (N. Gregory Mankiw. Principles of Macroeconomics, c. 2008)." Consumers demand goods and services and suppliers provide them at a price. Consumers buy them at the right price. This is called the Law of Supply and Demand. Capitalism allows for several vendors to offer a variety of products and services, and these vendors give consumers the free choice to decide what products and services to buy from whom at any given price.

A supplier might provide steak. Another vendor provides pork. A supplier might provide a brand new car. There are vendors that provide used cars. There might be a high quality stereo on the market that uses the latest sound technology, but there are other stereo systems that can provide a similar quality with cheaper components. Capitalism is designed to give people free choices to have the things they need or want within their price ranges. Competition insures that what the buyer can afford to pay and what the supplier charges remains at an equilibrium. Competition also insures that the consumer is getting the best quality products and services for the money. This is why some businesses fail while others succeed. The Law of Supply and Demand is working.

Consumers make decisions based on quality, need, and satisfaction. If a similar product is offered that provides the same benefits for a lower price, people will generally choose to pay the lower price. The "invisible hand" hand of the free market drives capitalism, and it is the catalyst for prosperity, which leads to the fullness of "...life, liberty, and the pursuit of happiness." It is also the heart of the American Spirit, driven by inventiveness, ingenuity, and hard work. It is not controlled by government. Businesses may manufacture and sell as much as they want at a price that the market will bear. The more need there is for a product or service, the more employees are needed to provide it. So, unemployment stays low. As a result, everyone shares in the benefits, and the quality of life, in general, is high for the nation as a whole.

In capitalism, there is no limit to prosperity as long as vendors provide a good product that does what it's supposed to do. Capitalism is the driving force of the economy.

Command Economy: Socialism and Communism

A command economy is when a government entity controls the economy of a nation. It owns the resources, manufacturing companies, controls the price, quantity, and quality of the products and services offered. Resources are limited, and since the manufacturing companies are owned by the government, there's a limit to the employees. The more limited the resources are, the higher the price. The quality of the products may be low, as well as the quantity. Unemployment is high, and the quality of life in the nation is low.

Since the government provides everything the nation needs, it produces what it believes the nation needs, and then sells it to the public. Utilities, phone, cars, clothes, food, and housing are all provided. The government sets the price, and people don't have a choice since there is no competition. Since there is a limit to the resources, governments must put a cap on production, and penalize people for using or buying too much. In theory, everyone is equal in a command economy, and everyone is supposed to have an allocation according to perceived needs. In an economically perfect world, this model would work. People would only use what is necessary, and there would be no need for caps and taxes to control it. However, not all people are the same. They have a variety of tastes, needs, wants, desires, and dreams. In a command economy, this variety is not provided. The government says, "We make it. You buy it. That's all you get." It is a law providing false weights and measures to steal from the general public.

God commanded his people in Deuteronomy 25:13-15, **"You will not**

15

have in your bag different weights, great and small. You will not have in your house different measures, great and small. You will have a perfect and just weight, a perfect and just measure you will have: that your days may be lengthened in the land which the Lord your God gives you." In those days, people were nomadic. They utilized free trade, and traveled to buy and sell goods. When they bought goods, they brought them to their homes and sold them on a street market or from their homes. God wanted them to understand that it was wrong to use dishonest business practices. Cap and trade is a law that legalizes dishonest business practices through the use of taxes to impose false weights and measures for certain companies, groups, individuals, and the government. In verse 16, it goes on to say that God hates it and will punish those who practice it.

A caste system develops so that the wealthy control the economy. As they allocate resources to the individuals they serve, they partake in privileges that would not be extended to someone else. They often take the best for themselves, and build nice houses, buy nice cars, wear top designer clothing, live in the comfort of the unlimited use of electricity and gas, and ration out the rest to the others. A common citizen must have permission from the government to go outside the borders for the purposes of commerce, but often, it is denied. Certain individuals are treated preferentially based upon hierarchical control within the favored wealthy groups. The favored wealthy often steal good ideas from their citizens and realize a profit from it themselves, taking the credit. Common citizens won't try anything, because they know it won't get them anywhere. In India, according to the Los Angeles Times in an article dated April 12, 1991, love between a man in a higher caste and a woman of a lower caste was discovered, and the penalty was death by hanging. When they refused to die, they were burned to death. They're stuck. There's no way out.

Capitalism is designed to prevent this from happening.

Monopoly and Taxes

The above is what is called an oligopoly. It is a government controlled economy that monopolizes the resources. A monopoly is one or a few entities that offer the same products and services. They set the prices, and the consumer pays it. Since there is a cap on the use of resources, then production is limited. The cap is utilized by taxing a company on its profits. People have to make a decision to pay a certain amount of money within their budgets, and they must include the tax. So, often, they don't buy enough of goods and services to satisfy their needs. If they need more, then they are penalized with an additional tax, which may be accompanied by a fees or surcharges for using more than the allocated amount. The company is charged the taxes and the fees, but then passes those taxes and fees to the consumer.

The controversial cap and trade bill introduced by the White House in 2009 will do this. It attempts to create monopoly companies by limiting production, taxing the price above equilibrium, and then it will penalize individuals for using too much. The government is attempting regulate a natural law, which is not possible. The result is that certain companies will be favored to operate over others, and subsidized while possible competition is drowned out. Other initiatives include forcing common people to take public transportation when it is necessary to have private transportation, raising use tax on utilities and penalizing for using beyond the allocated amounts, raising the tax on fuels and cheapening their values, and raising the tax on products that we need to have on a daily basis, such as food and water.

For years, by the way, this has been leading to a "nanny state," in which all aspects of human life are monitored and controlled, from the jobs we work, to the food we eat, to the people we befriend, to the living arrangements we make for ourselves, and the clothes we wear. Look at the good and robust health of American citizens only 50 years ago. Compare them to today. We are skinny and weak. My hat is off to you, Office of the Surgeon General. From abortion to diet, you contributed to the defeat of America. I hope it's not too late.

If a government out-of-control can't stop us, it will regulate us. If that doesn't work, it will give us the wrong education. If that doesn't work, it will starve us. If that doesn't work, it will kill us! Something's bound to work! It's all done in the name of protecting the consumer. The only people it really protects is the wealthy and those who govern.

History has made it clear to us. As voiced by President Vladimir Putin in an article by PA Pundits called, "Putin: Obama "Idiot" for Adopting Socialism. He states:

"Any fourth grade history student knows socialism has failed in every country, at every time in history," said Putin. "President Obama and his fellow Democrats are either idiots or deliberately trying to destroy

CHAPTER FIVE
STATIC MATHEMATICS VERSUS PERPETUAL MOTION

A History of Derivatives

Investors wanted some idea of how and when to invest their money to make the greatest profit. An investor who can find the trends can make a lot of money. The derivative was developed to attempt to predict trends of an economic entity.

Derivatives are used, in general, to determine what it costs to acquire materials, make a product, pay the utilities, pay employees, and how much of the product to sell to pay the bills and wages to break-even. When the break-even point is found, the derivative is used to determine how much of the product to sell at various prices to make a profit. Other factors are considered, such as availability of resources, competition, and past performance of the company. The formula is also used to predict how much of a product can be made and sold before it will lose money. In a vacuum, with no other factors to consider, derivatives work perfectly. An investor can get an accurate view of the company's future performance by looking at past performance. For short term results, derivatives can be used to accurately predict the profitability of a company for no longer than a year.

The problem is that the economy and the world are not perfect. Even though there would be no reason to believe that a company would fail, things happen. Market conditions change, products go obsolete, a competitor makes a better product, accidents take place, employees change jobs, people stop buying the product for one reason or another, suppliers run out of resources, and buyers may switch suppliers. For this reason, derivatives are not long term.

According to Frontline in a video interview with Terri Duhon, employee of JP Morgan from 1994 to 2002 titled "Derivatives", credit derivatives were used in futures trading and hedge funds to guarantee a return for an investment regardless of the price of a commodity. Even though it is high risk, people were attracted to it because of the high returns. The way it was sold, they understood that they would not lose their principal and additional insurance was purchased to protect the capital, and the investment fund would continue to grow. JP Morgan formed with third party financial institutions to transfer some of the credit risk to free up capital to lend, which allowed them to carry less debt on their balance sheets, fulfilling regulatory requirements.

Every economist knows that the more of a product that is used, the more that is produced. Due to the nature of manufacturing and processing, the more that is sold, the less it costs to produce. When cost goes down, so does the price to maintain equilibrium. Lesser quantities of a product are purchased, lesser quantities are produced. Therefore, if less of a product is sold, then it costs more to produce. When costs go up, so does the price. It was great when people were buying oil in great quantities at lower prices. People stopped buying as much oil, and it drove the price up. Derivatives assumed a relatively study price with an assumed percentage of growth. Brokers guaranteed a high return to their investors. When people started cashing in, the money wasn't there, and oil shot up to twice as much as is today. Derivatives were also used for other investments and weak mortgage loans, packaged together, and guaranteed to bring a high rate of return. The use of derivatives was responsible for the economic crisis that almost bankrupted the world banking system.

The use of the derivative formulas are static in nature, and should only be used in the beginning stages of a company to determine if it might become profitable. They should only be used to determine the break-even point and the height of profit based on current market conditions. They are used for hypotheses, and no more. They are static equations, which cannot be used in a perpetual motion economy, and must be adjusted as market conditions change.

CHAPTER SIX
CAPITALISM AND CHARITY

The Law of Conservation: You can't get something for nothing

The universe operates on the dynamics of the three laws of motion.

- ☐ **Law One: A body at rest will stay at rest and a body in motion will remain in motion in a straight line unless interrupted by resistance.**

- ☐ **Law Two: For every action, there is an equal and opposite reaction.**

- ☐ **Law Three: It takes force to produce force.**

If a car is at rest, it will remain at rest until someone starts it and presses the accelerator for it to move. The car will continue to move in a straight line unless it is steered or stopped. Movement is impossible without force.

Motion is only possible when some external force exerts itself upon an object, and it then becomes inertia that does work. According to Isaac Asimov in, "Understanding Physics," that the Latin term "inertia" is used to describe rest and work. Inertia means "laziness," or unused potential.

If the universe operates on these laws, then most certainly, the economy does. The third law is also called the law of conservation. It means that to get something, it requires action. That action will cause a reaction that will hopefully produce something. The farmer has to sow seeds, water it, and weed it. The field will go into motion to produce fruit. A field that lays empty won't grow crops.

A man cannot be expected to work without payment. On the other hand, a man cannot expect to get paid without doing work. The same principal applies to money. Should the bank loan money if there isn't sufficient income to make the payments? It's a violation of the law of conservation. You can't get something for nothing.

Capitalism and the laws of motion work hand-in-hand. Since

capitalism is based upon the free will and pioneering spirit of mankind, then responsibility for action rests upon mankind. Therefore, a man "at rest" will tend to remain at rest if he has no will to move. Many people use rationalize that since they believe in God, things will just automatically happen for them. They believe that God will bring them prosperity.

In Genesis 1:25-30, God gave mankind dominion over the whole of the earth. Moses, the author, specifies in verse 28, that God instructed Adam,

"...Be fruitful and multiply, and replenish the earth, and subdue it: and have dominion over the fish of the sea, and over the fowl of the air, and over every living thing that moveth upon the earth."

In verse 29, it says,

"And God said, Behold, I have given you every herb bearing seed, which is upon the face of the earth, and every tree, in the which is the fruit of a tree yielding seed; to you it shall be for meat."

At that time, before sin, mankind was vegetarian. The earth was designed to be a self-sufficient eco-system that would provide for mankind.

How did God provide for us? We have to work the earth. The earth can't cultivate itself. Every plant and tree that provided fruit also provided a seed, so that resources can be replenished when they are used. In order to eat, it is necessary to pick the fruit and herbs. If Adam wanted these fruits and herbs in a more localized area, he would have to take the seed there, plant it, tend to it, and it would grow to bear fruit. It had to be earned. Earning it meant working to provide for needs. It was his responsibility.

While it is true that God provided for us everything we need to survive, replenish the earth, and be strong enough to have dominion over the earth, it is not true that He will bring it to us. We have to find it, obtain it, maintain it, and then we can enjoy the fruits of our labor. There is no other way. We can enjoy as much as we can maintain, and have as much as we want. That is the way of capitalism: find it, obtain it, maintain it, and enjoy the fruits of your labor. This is why the Jews are so successful in working Israel's farm land. If anyone else occupied the land, it would turn to desert because of a lack of knowledge. When the Jews are in Israel, the land thrives. They know how to work it so that it will bring fruit. You can't get something for nothing.

Charity is just a messed up word. In I Corinthians 13, faith, hope and charity are spoken of. Charity, in this context, doesn't mean giving money, clothes, or your time. That's only PART of the meaning. Charity, in this context, means love. I don't think anyone really understands what love really is, but I can tell you this, that love is a decision, it doesn't move very easily, it doesn't easily anger, and it is the drive behind a person to do good things. If I give money, but my drive isn't love, it's worthless. If I give clothes, but have no love, its vanity. If I sacrifice my life, but have no love, it was a waste of a life. Love doesn't give up. I don't know of any love such as this . . . it is too great for me to comprehend. And, I know that God operates in love, even in His wrath. This, also, is too great for me to understand.

Charity: A Great Fallacy

Today's meaning of charity is to give of your substance to take care of the poor. It has been argued that this is the way to take care of the poor without having anything to do with them. You don't need love to do it. You just haphazardly find some outlet that will take your money and use it to feed and clothe the poor.

I remember a day that I was SO embarrassed. I had been trying to find work. I was using the library to seek for work, apply for jobs, and paying a dime a page for resumes that I made. I was out of money, out of gas, and hungry. I went to a soup kitchen, and stood in line. A woman drove up, and got a bunch of meat and other food items out of the trunk, and took it in to the woman that had a staff to cook it and serve it to us. I wasn't exactly dressed like a prince, and when she looked at me, I smiled at her, meaning to thank her for what she did. She looked at me in disgust, and ran to her car in fear. I don't know what she thought, but I meant to show a small sign of gratitude, which was rejected. I can't eat in sorrow. It was bad enough that I was there to begin with. I lost my appetite, and went home. This lady canceled out her own blessing, because her motivation for giving was not based upon love. There is no fear in love. She should never have given anything at all.

The other problem with charity is that people have forgotten that the poor have a responsibility. There is a pretty familiar quote that's popular among the impoverished. "The wealthy are responsible to insure the needs of the poor are met." I think most of the wealthy take this responsibility seriously, however, the way in which they do so is by opening businesses, training people, and paying them for an honest day's work. That is capitalism.

22

Those who believe in charity forget that people have to work for their own subsistence. The only people who don't have to work are those who are invalids, handicapped, and mentally retarded. Most people on welfare, today, are not handicapped. They are able bodied people capable of working, but are laden with excuses for not doing so. Sometimes, there are doctors that allow them to carry these excuses, and oblige them with a false diagnosis. This is socialism. It's a welfare state that provides no motivation for self-betterment. It is money wasted. No services are provided, no products are being produced, and the Gross National Product and Gross Domestic Product goes down. Deficits become greater because money is being poured into a great vacuum we call "the poor." It's a waste.

I owned my own business, once. I went to a homeless shelter run by a church to hire some people to canvas an area for $6.00 an hour. They accepted the job. I showed them the money to insure them that they would be paid for their work. When I went to pick them up the next day, one of them said that a doctor told him that he had a "growth" in his lymph nodes and that he should rest and not work. It was an excuse to remain under the care of the shelter, and to never be self-sufficient. The other one didn't have an excuse, but wanted to stay with his friend. I had money. I was willing to pay. They had no excuse. They wanted me to just give it to them without expecting them to earn it. In order for me to be successful, I needed workers. The church was acting as a rehabilitation facility, as well. Its function was to house the impoverished, educate them, set them up to be interviewed by employers, and send them out to be successes. The "ministry" was ineffective. The police struck a deal with the pastor to drop off homeless people, many of whom were criminals. This is not the purpose of the church. This is a perfect example of the government using religion for its own purposes. It's socialism. I'm not a socialist. I don't give money to able bodied people who haven't worked for it.

This book, for instance, is work. So, when I spend money to produce it, advertise it, send out copies, and ask for money to keep it going, I think it is right to expect a return. I worked for it. I didn't beg for the money to produce the book. It's a valid opinion that I think is worth the money to buy. So, as far as I'm concerned, when media outlets and politicians obtain copies of the book for free, it's stealing. If you're so interested in my opinion, then pay for it. I have to make a living. So, you want me to give to your causes? Buy and promote the book. It's that simple. I can't work in a vacuum.

It's the law of conservation, and the universe operates in it. It takes force to produce force. In the case of hiring someone to canvas, money was the force that usually provides the motivation for a man to work. If you provide a good service, I will pay you. Then, hopefully, you will provide that service again, and I will pay you, again. The idea was to keep making money so that I could pay a wage to people who helped me. I was rejected. So, I kept my money and canvassed the area myself, because people in that city needed a cattle prod. I couldn't find anyone who was willing to work for the money. I couldn't be successful because I was doing all the work myself. I couldn't keep up with it. You can't get something for nothing

CHAPTER SEVEN
ILLEGAL IMMIGRATION, CORPORATE ABUSE, AND MINIMUM WAGE

Old Testament Israel and the United States: A Comparison

Jeremiah, an Old Testament prophet of the Bible, didn't have any desire to "rock the boat." However, through a succession of circumstances, pain, and the deadly disposition of his own country, he was forced to preach the words of God, in the great hopes that the people of Israel might repent of their sins. At one point in time, Jeremiah wrote in his book Jeremiah 20:8, 9a, and 14 that he cursed the day he was born, and didn't want to make any mention of God. In verse 9b, he says, "But his word was in mine heart as a burning fire shut up in my bones, and I was weary with forbearing, and I could not stay." Jeremiah was full of the words of God. They were the driving force for his anger, and he wrote in verse 11, "But the Lord is with me as a mighty terrible one: therefore my persecutors shall stumble, and they shall not prevail: they shall be greatly ashamed; for they shall not prosper: their everlasting confusion shall never be forgotten."

Jeremiah was only a child when the Lord ordered him to carry out His word. Jeremiah resisted the call, because of his youth, but the Lord told him in chapter 1:8, "...I am with thee to deliver thee." The Lord told him that he was going to bring a foreign nation to destroy Israel and to take his people into captivity.

Ezekiel was called, as well, to preach a similar message approximately 35 years later. The Lord told him in Ezekiel 3:26, not to speak a work to them, and to not reprove them of their evil deeds, "...for they are a rebellious house." The Lord would use him as a mouthpiece, and speak through him, saying, "Thus saith the Lord God; He that heareth, let him hear; and he that forbeareth, let him forbear: for they are a rebellious house."

In this day, it seems that the Lord Himself is speaking all over the world, as in Isaiah 1:2, "Hear, O heavens, and give ear, O earth: for the Lord hath spoken, I have nourished and brought up children, and they have rebelled against me. The ox knoweth his owner, and the ass his master's crib: but Israel doth not know, my people doth not

consider." When God made the Old Testament covenant with Israel, the people agreed to the blessings for living under the statutes of the Lord, and the punishments for straying from the statutes. In Deuteronomy 28:1and 2, the Lord makes the promises concerning the blessings: **"...if thou shalt hearken diligently unto the voice of the Lord thy God, to observe and to do all his commandments which I command thee this day, that the Lord thy God will set thee on high above all nations of the earth: And all these blessings shall come on thee, and overtake thee, if thou shalt hearken unto the voice of the Lord thy God."** The list of blessings is from verse 2 through 13. The punishments are listed from chapter 28:14 through chapter 29:29. Within these verses, one of the punishments is that strangers will rise in power. They will become the blessed ones, and they will lead, lend, and destroy the country, taking prisoner the residents who will become slaves.

The United States is a nation borne of God. There is nothing going on in the United States that has not been spoken in the books of Isaiah, Jeremiah, and Ezekiel. These books are available separately at your Christian bookstore. There is no sense in telling you things that have already been written. I'm not here to reprove anyone's deeds, either. The message, though, is "WAKE UP AND SMELL THE COFFEE." Anyone who reads this is well familiar with right and wrong, and has heard the words of God. He's done talking. He's issued the warnings, and no one listened. What is happening today,   from Hurricane Katrina, the two Persian Gulf wars, the British Petroleum oil spill, to the unbearable ice storms, floods, and unprecedented numbers of tornadoes ripping through the United States, is the wrath of God.

Get a clue.

Illegal Immigrants and cheap labor: Do American workers expect too much?

People that are useful in their occupations such as finance, carpentry, landscaping, farming, and general labor are important people. When the Pilgrims first came here, they built farms, houses, retail outlets, developed a system of credit, and built strong communities with teachers that were willing to teach children how to read, write, and do math. Each family had a specific trade they specialized in, which was carried down to the children who ran the family business. Working families are the foundation of the United States. The women worked as hard as the men, and when the children were old enough to do chores and work, they worked as hard as the adults. There might have been restaurants, but there really wasn't a need for them. The best restaurant in town was at home, and Mom was the head cook. Hard working, down to earth, at home people built this nation. Without them, there would be no need of a banker, a police officer, a mayor, a governor, or a president. There would be no need of senators and representatives. Without them, there would be no nation.

With the invention of convenient transportation, people began moving out of the local areas, and living anywhere but home. Very few parents, today, are handing down their businesses to their children, even though the businesses were meant to provide a living for themselves and future generations. There are very few farm families, who had to sell their farms to corporations, who now tend to them. The family may work for the corporations, or may have had to find another line of work. Things change, and that's OK. I'm all for change, as long as it provides a higher benefit. It is my opinion that a younger generation giving up its heritage is wrong. The vocations that their fathers worked in are the building blocks of America that keep on building. To abandon those building blocks is to unravel the sewing that holds the country together.

In a microwave generation, corporate farming has become the norm; restaurants are more common, because people don't cook. Our food is planted, picked, peeled, packaged, and made available to us at the grocery store. Our clothes are made outside the United States, and imported. We don't build our own houses, anymore. A hand-made wedding gown is not handed down from mother to daughter; it's bought from a store. Electricity powers everything from lights to power tools, and gas heats our houses and cooks our dinner. Even cars are made with international parts. There is truly nothing that is American made.

These things aren't bad things. I think that we should live in comfort. I don't have a problem with that, but generations X and Y have both taken for granted our wonderful blessings. What exactly would we do if, in an instant, electricity was no longer available? What if oil companies stopped producing oil to provide gas to heat our homes? What if corporate America casts off farming and we now have to cultivate the earth on our own to feed ourselves? Would we be able to make our own clothes? Can we go into a forest, chop down a couple of trees and build a house? Can we plow the fields with a couple of horses or oxen? Can we build carts and silos to store the grain in? The ability to do such things was the building blocks of communities, towns, cities, counties, and states. There was once a great pride in saying, "I made that," or "I grew that," or "I built that." I know that I am one of those people who could not survive without these services that are provided for me. I'm just now appreciating planting seeds, watching plants grow, and bloom with very little work involved. Weed it once a week, water it, and spray it for bugs. It's amazing that some flowers will produce 100 times more seed than was planted for one plant. If I want the same type of flowers next year, I don't have to spend any money buying seeds to plant. I can harvest the seeds, instead, and plant them. It was once a tradition for a newlywed couple to have a house built for them by the community without charge. The man was given farm land to cultivate to provide for his family and aid in the support of the community. This is no longer the case.

Generation X is nearly incapable of any of it. People are looked down upon for not driving cars. So what's wrong with walking, riding a bike, or taking the bus? Unless you are an Olympic athlete training, walking or riding a bike means that you can't get a license, so you must be an ex-con. Running means that you committed a crime. Taking the bus is equivalent to being on welfare. What happened to our pride?

It would seem that we have become too good for labor. So, we look for someone to do the labor for us, and there is no one who is available. Where do we go? We find illegal aliens. They have trade skills in the areas of carpentry, plumbing, tiling, painting, framing, roofing, and landscaping. These are highly coveted skills. Yet, Americans seem to be too good to do it. And if they do the hard work, they'll want to be paid a great deal more than an illegal alien, who is just trying to survive, often on contracted amounts far below average. Two and three families are supported in a small house or an apartment, while the men work. I have seen fifteen people in one household, and three men working for half the wage of one man, and still feeding everyone in the house without electricity or gas. They'll pay for water, but that's it. They're relatively happy.

I don't get it. An American on welfare loses the air conditioning and you're asking for a fight. Where did America go wrong? I think American standards are too high, and there are no men who can fix a car, paint a house, install a light fixture, or landscape. That's below us. We have illegal aliens to do that, for cheap. Isn't it a matter of national security that Americans be able to do these things? Shouldn't we, as Americans, be hiring Americans to do these jobs?

Minimum wage laws frustrate American Employers

Every year, there seems to be a debate about minimum wage. This was for teenagers and those just leaving home. If they were on time, worked smart, worked hard, and brought a profit to the company for their hard work, then they were awarded with a raise. If they stayed on the job, they were awarded with a promotion with a raise. If they stayed for a while, then they were able to put themselves in a position to retire, and perhaps change careers for a second retirement. At the age of 65, they were able to retire.

Paying someone to work in a starting position for any more than minimum wage was ridiculous. I agree that there should be a minimum wage. I also believe that there should be a starting wage paid to reflect education and experience. However, I don't believe that minimum wage for unskilled laborers should be any more than five dollars and fifty cents an hour. Today's minimum wage is seven dollars and twenty five cents an hour. Congress is debating over whether it should be increased again. Moreover, companies are being forced to pay for benefits, such as health care and vision.

Companies are in business to make money. While I believe that it is the owner's responsibility to provide a safe environment, equipment to do the job, and to give time off for their employees when they are sick, I believe that health care is the sole responsibility of the employee. Companies should not have to pay for half of it, though they should provide information on how to get health care insurance. Employees should be encouraged to get health care insurance. The employee is responsible to save for medical emergencies, or any other type of emergency. Employees should not be living above their means. They should be able to pay their rent, utilities, buy any old used car with cash with just liability insurance, and put gas in it. If they want more, they should get a second job. It's called financial planning.

The federal government is requiring companies to provide everything for the employee. Since companies have to make a profit to operate, they must obey the law of conservation, and cut costs where necessary without compromising products and services. Training costs money. If a starting employee is trained, but doesn't make the cut, that's a waste of money. A training-to-proficiency ratio is for every 100 trainees, only 10 will become proficient, and only 1 will remain for any length of time. Employers look for qualified people to begin with, then, and save money in training costs. They can pay employees what they are worth, and save time and money. They might throw in benefits, but today, one qualified employee is as good as ten unqualified employees. Why spend all that money on someone that's not going to work out?

Since illegal aliens are not documented workers, they do not fit under the American labor laws. Hiring them means that the company can reach its goals by paying half the wage, saving taxes, and getting good skilled labor for the money paid. Illegal aliens won't say anything about getting paid less, because they'll be deported. If they want to work again, well, they have to provide good products and services. This is how they make their living, without complaint.

American Mediocrity: Earning a day's wages

Today's American won't do the work and expect a paycheck. There's a belt buckle that reads, "I want less work, more weekend, and more money for doing it." It might explain the BP oil spill, the Enron and Madoff scandals, the Wall Street scandals, AIG, Freddie Mac, and Fannie Mae. People want more money with less responsibility, without providing quality services in honesty and integrity. Services provided by Americans are mediocre at best, and is the reason companies don't hire them. I met a guy who told me that he has to hire illegal aliens, because they work without complaint. All others need a ride, want food brought to them, want to be treated with respect, and then still won't do the job right.

Will the United States repeat history?

We shouldn't live in the past, but we shouldn't forget history. I've shown you the history of Israel from the fifth century BC. The books I cited match word for word the disgraceful behaviors of the people in America. It is for these same behaviors that God punished Israel and several other nations in history. If the people of the United States forget, then it will fall as the others. It's inevitable. It's happening before our eyes. Current events dictate man-made disasters, terrorism, illegal alien insurgencies, natural disasters, parents killing their own children, and children invading schools and shooting their fellow students and teachers. This was all told in the Old Testament, and it is a forewarning to us. Read the Lamentations of Jeremiah. Then read Joel. I promise you, everything that is happening today is in those books.

I'm an unwilling preacher. Nevertheless, "Repent." Return to the Lord your God that He may restore you to your rightful position.

CHAPTER 8
TO BE OR NOT TO BE? OR BOTH?
OIL OR ALTERNATIVE ENERGY? A COMPROMISE.

Drilling and the EPA: The Big Six works with the Federal Government

According to a research management plan by the staff of Texas A and M University, a partnership was formed to "develop environmentally friendly drilling practices in the oil and gas industry." Noble technology Services, Houston Advanced Research Council, and the Department of Petroleum Engineering studied new and unproven drilling technologies for the purposes of integrating them for use in off-limits areas such as Otero Basins of New Mexico, coastal margins of Texas, Louisiana, Alabama, Mississippi and in the desert.

These co-ops are working in conjunction with the US Department of Energy, utilizing the Drilling Waste Management Information System. Studies have shown the benefits of direction drilling, or using one surface hole to drill several wells at one time, as in the THUMS operations on four man-made islands off the coast of Long Beach, California. 1200 wells have been drilled, and according to the fact sheet, "Drilling Practices That Minimize Generation of Drilling Wastes," 720 wells were drilled utilizing the other 480. In conventional drilling, there would have been a farm of 1200 oil wells that would have taken up a lot of land. The use of directional drilling minimized the use of land for platforms, and protected the environment, while drawing oil from several shelves on different levels below the earth's surface. It eliminates strip mining, an environmental disaster that destroys entire eco-systems that can throw the balance of nature off.

The Environmental Protection Agency also created stricter guidelines for waste emissions and required that oil companies recycle the waste for reuse, and then eject the cleaned and harmless unusable waste into the ocean. It also demanded the same type of recycling for land wells, which produces a kind of mulch that can be used to fertilize farm land.

Why only US companies should be drilling on US land and

coastlines

Americans understand the importance of natural resources. They also understand the importance of working the earth, and handing down a heritage from their ancestry to their children so that they can make a living. Americans understand that they are a unique people with a unique identification that sets them apart from all others. This uniqueness is not necessarily a desirable trait to other nations, but it is what makes America work. Americans realize just how important it is to be on the front line of all trades to harvest the blessings of their labors. Furthermore, it is Americans that have been studying safer drilling practices since 1969, when Santa Barbara was destroyed by defective sheathing in the drilling tube.

It is in the best interest of the United States to continue building oil rigs to drill for oil off the coast lines. We should not allow a disaster such as BP to stop us. This is why I believe that the Alaskan the Gulf of Mexico oil spills were the result of owners and CEO's neglecting their duties to maintain the rigs on American property. I'm sure that they cared about the profits, but had little regard for the environment or the people that worked for them.

I do not believe that from this time forward, that foreign entities should own American businesses. It is only Americans that understand the importance of American natural resources. And it is Americans that will provide the best work possible under American ownership. It is a matter of national security. Furthermore, domestic owners are more likely to protect their assets at home more efficiently than they will protect them elsewhere. It is good for border security, as well, since these areas would be United States government property via private entities. America has the right to protect and defend itself and its resources against terrorists, and can stop illegal immigrants from crossing, whether swimming, traveling by boat or submarine. Offshore drilling and border security share a common interest.

It's also a matter of national security that we should be putting our navy and air force in charge of protecting our offshore oil rigs. I am convinced that not only did BP fail to comply with safety standards in maintaining their American located oil rigs, but that the oil well five miles below the surface was attacked by a terrorist entity. Union oil in 1969 failed to comply with safety standards to install superior sheathing in the drill tubes to shortcut the process. As a result, a drilling tube broke while 193 million

33

gallons of oil spilled onto the coasts of Santa Barbara, causing millions of dollars of damage.

In an investigation of the BP Horizon rig explosion concerning the sheathing of the drill tube under the surface. One of the reasons that the explosion occurred was that when the rig was built, sub-standard sheathing was installed. My guess is that inspectors were paid to ignore safety violations in drilling, as it was found with Union Oil in 1969. As a result, Union Oil was broken into six subdivisions, and Exxon-Mobile became the largest provider of oil in the country, if not the world. I believe that Americans have learned from the Santa Barbara disaster. Other countries drilling in the United States could really care less.

BP forgot history, and should be forced to abandon operations in America, and its coastal areas. Forget litigation. Forget spending millions of dollars to penalize and jail people. BP should be forced to hand ownership of these wells to American businessmen in the oil trade and denied any profit from the operations of these wells. BP will more than pay for their mistakes by sacrificing their heritage in oil in America to provide the same heritage to Americans to replace what they lost. There should also be an investigation of the other four companies that built the platform, drilled the hole, provided the pumps, and installed the pipeline. If one or more are found to be guilty, then they should be paying as well. This wasn't entirely BP's fault, but on the other hand, they own the lion's share of the profits coming from that well. If the companies that were sub-contracted to provide the labor and the equipment, and BP failed to maintain it, then the liability rests solely upon BP.

Oil is not going away. Who other than Americans should make money on it? We are fools if we don't. If we don't, someone else will, and that is a threat to national security.

Solar, Wind, and Nuclear Power

The sun is another God-given resource that we are free to use for our own benefit. Solar panels are used with deep-cell batteries to provide electricity. People use them to power their entire houses, individual appliances, or water heaters. If the panels are built and installed, the power of the sun can be used for free. While it is true that it provides no corporate interest in that individuals can get utilities on their own, it frees up available income to spend elsewhere. This is why I don't agree with laws stating that people must buy their utilities from an electric company.

I even believe that if individuals can pump their own water, purify it, and have it for personal consumption; they can save money on the water bill, and the billing rates. However, most cities have water and mineral rights. A man in Colorado was forced to shut down his well because it was against the law for him to have it. That's preposterous. It's his land, and the water was in his well.

Wind is another resource that we may freely use to our benefit. Individuals should be free to build their own machines to create electricity for their houses. If a person can put up a windmill in his own backyard and generate his own electricity, why should he have to pay someone else? If he's generating it for his own use, then it's nobody's business. It's when he sells it that he needs a license.

Nuclear power is another good alternative. It's dangerous. It's risky. It produces nuclear waste materials. However, there must be a way to refine nuclear waste for use in generating power for other things, such as cars, boats, and motorcycles. Not all nuclear waste is waste. It might be a waste product of the factory; however, it can be recycled. No one seems to have taken the time to figure out what to do with it. I have a sneaking suspicion that people have already devised a way to use it, but haven't developed the technology. The blueprints are sitting in a backroom, somewhere. Perhaps it is now practical to send nuclear waste into space in a pressurized, reusable capsule to be emptied.   Then, it should be cleaned at a space laboratory, prior to being brought back on a transport. Or, being that we know some of the elements that are in space, and that they can be attached to nuclear waste to make it reusable, we can bring that renewed waste back here and reuse it.

Oil and Alternative Energy: A partnership

Oil and alternative energy must be partners. One cannot be sustained without the other. Oil is needed to lubricate parts. Gas is needed to run the processing plants. Oil is needed for many plastics that we make from it. Even though countries may switch to alternative energy, there will still be a demand for it. There's already some complaint that hybrid cars are just too quiet, and they are dangerous for the blind, a complaint that has no consequence. The blind are usually not out on the sidewalks, and if they are, they have seeing eye-dogs, or they have friends and family that watch out for them. The blind also have naturally sharpened their other senses and have memorized their walking routes. They use a stick marked red so that others will know they are blind. Drivers see these and can avoid hitting them. This is simply not an issue. A blind person can hear the quietest mouse tip-toeing across the dining room floor from a bedroom across the house.

Being that the profits of big oil are so huge, then it only makes sense to invest a percentage of the profits into the alternative energy market. Oil and natural energy can be used hand-in-hand. Ten percent of the world's oil profits would be enough to get workable, reliable, and safe solar, wind, and nuclear power to work for us. Hybrid cars are a good partnership, since the gas tank is only ten gallons, and it takes one tank to travel from San Antonio to Oklahoma City. Conventional gas cars use two 15 gallon tanks, if they are six cylinder engines. Eight cylinder engines take three tanks.

Aside of the British Petroleum rig, the Heritage, blowing up in the Gulf of Mexico, oil is an important export product. Governor Jindal stressed that when the fishing industry is down, people work for oil companies on the rigs. It is alternative employment so that they can support themselves and their families. A six month moratorium on oil drilling is preposterous. There are several other rigs, 32, in the Gulf of Mexico, that are safe. If there is to be a temporary freeze on oil drilling, it cannot be all at once for such a long period of time. One oil well at a time can be manned with a skeleton crew while inspections are done. It certainly shouldn't take any longer than a week to get a team to inspect one well. People should not be out of work any longer than necessary. The fishing industry is dried up because of the oil spill. Why punish the innocent for something they didn't do? Repair the oil rig and put it back into operation.

CHAPTER 9
THE WILL OF THE PEOPLE OR THE WILL OF THE ELITE?

United States funding of Special Interest Groups: Special Interest Groups create Elitism

"Elite" is defined as a small group of influential people. It might be a group of corporate executives in a company, a group made up of wealthy people, or a group of thugs. Totalitarianism is a small group of elites that impose legislation on large masses of people. A special interest group can become an elite group that imposes legislation on the masses without informing the masses. A good example is when Congress passed a law that forced all networks to switch to High Definition television (HDTV) broadcasting. No one knew that the law had been passed until February of 2007. Notices were put on the shelves of department stores that in February of 2009, HDTV was the law. I still question that this had been imposed upon us without representation. I didn't particularly want to switch over to HDTV. I won't always have cable, and the cable that was already offered was crystal clear. I always made use of the two or three channels that were broadcast that didn't need special programming. I was denied the choice. So, now, we have to pay more for something that doesn't really make any difference. We don't have a choice. If we want to watch TV, then we have to pay for the supposedly clearer broadcast signal. It's an example of the totalitarian elite imposing law for its own benefit. Why, exactly, do we need HDTV? No one has explained it, other than, "Everyone in communications is switching to it." Why?

I understand the need for some special interest groups such as the Pro-Life movement, groups that stand for religious freedom and citizen "watchdogs" that keep tabs on our representative government. It is absolutely important that we respect life, speak for those who cannot speak for themselves, and to insure that separate life forming in the womb is recognized as human life rather than what some groups say is just a "tumor." It is important for us to understand that God provided us a nation that facilitates the free publishing of the Gospel (the intent), as well as the freedom of people to choose their own paths of life according to their own conscience and belief systems, so long as these religions do not impede upon the belief systems of others and violate the human rights of those belonging to another religion. It is important that watchdog groups keep tabs on our government to insure that groups of people, religious organizations, or representatives are not overstepping their Constitutional boundaries that protect our freedoms. Additionally, I believe that watchdog groups should be tax free since monies given to them to support their causes are free will gifts from people who have already paid taxes on that money.

However, though we have the freedom to choose to worship God or even gods and idols, we MUST understand that Christianity, first and foremost, reveals from the pages of the Bible (specifically the New Testament), the foundations of personal responsibility and morality. It provides the basic framework for Capitalism and God's intent for the maximum freedom of Mankind. Educated people understand that even if it isn't a Christian representation of God that we answer to some deity, such as the cosmos, in some shape or form. It is also understood that there is a low probability of a bunch of rag-tag rebels that barely survived the voyage from England to the United States and a near death in the winter would survive the highly organized armies of the Crown unless they had some kind of help from somewhere outside themselves. This rag-tag bunch of rebels had faith in God and Jesus Christ and believed in the destiny of the small beginnings of the nation to become a great institution of freedom from tyranny and oppression that people experience from their governments in other nations. Our nation fosters and strengthens the human spirit, encourages growth of individual intelligence, and lays down the framework for productivity and prosperity. The growth of any nation is reproduction of the species along with the principles handed down to the children. The children, then, take these principles and continue building. It is it in the family unit, the carrying down of traditions, in the transference of profession through parental guidance and training as well as organized education, basic morality, and in the teaching of Constitutional principles that the United States thrives.

Therefore, special interest groups that we need to support are those that specifically expose and fight policies that inhibit personal freedoms, fight corporations and elites that lobby for protections for union labor against non-union labor, and fight religion that puts itself above the Constitution. The Nation of Islam in America is a religion and special interest group that inhibits personal freedoms, supports unions, and raises their religious legal system above the Constitution of the United States – and must be fought.

Sharia Law vs. the Torah and the US Code of Law

So, at the peril of doing so, it is necessary to publish portions of Sharia Law and the Torah in Appendix B in order to continue to enlighten people that fundamentalist Islam in its current form, is unconstitutional, and is a violation of human rights and of freedom. It is a special interest group that must not receive federal funding of any type, and must not be allowed to encroach upon a free people with its totalitarian and oppressive laws that will literally boot a highly technological free society back to the 8th Century, dirt streets, grass huts, and poverty. Where are is an Islamic presence in the United States, there is poverty, crime, drugs, adult and child prostitution, black marketing, and an absolute hatred for Christians and Jesus Christ. I ought to know. I was a Christian living in these areas.

Planned Parenthood is another good example of a special interest group that should not receive funding at the federal level. The organization provides education on sexually transmitted diseases and their prevention as well as the prevention of unwanted pregnancies through birth control, as well as educating the general public on specific disorders that require birth control medication for women. However, Planned Parenthood has also become a part of the K-12 school system, advocating that should a teenage girl become pregnant, that the parents should not be informed of a decision to abort the child though the parents are responsible for their daughter and the life of the child inside. The male often doesn't pay anything, and may impregnate another teenage girl, which will warrant another parentally uninformed abortion at the counsel of a Planned Parenthood representative. It is a moral problem in the United States because in murder trials, when a pregnant woman is purposely harmed in some way as to cause a miscarriage, the person responsible for it is charged with murder. Similarly, if a woman is murdered while she is pregnant and it causes the death of the child inside her, the person responsible is charged with two murders. Yet, when two consenting teenagers or adults give themselves to one another, and the woman gets pregnant, Planned Parenthood asserts that it's perfectly legal to abort the pregnancy. The moral question is then, why is an unborn baby considered life prior to birth in one instance, and considered "just a tumor" in the other? Therefore, since federal funding to the agency is provided by the taxpayers regardless of state, it doesn't take into consideration the moral beliefs of those taxpayers. Therefore, it is a state issue. If the majority of the people abiding in that state are OK with abortion, then individual states should be providing the tax base at the state level, and not the federal level. This way, the individual states will be morally responsible for the consequences of murdering innocent souls who committed no crimes. Since when, I ask, is an innocent person responsible for the actions of another?

The Commission on Global Warming

Al Gore, the former Vice President of the United States under the Clinton administration, became the spokesman for environmental initiatives. International scientists studied the environment to predict global warming and to provide a solution to the problem. Al Gore spoke on behalf of the scientists representing the United Nations. He argued that carbon dioxide, the waste emission of animals (including humans) through exhaling, sweating, and belching was the main ingredient for "global warming."

However, if anyone has been to a basic biology class in high school, it's pretty clear that carbon monoxide (CO) is the reason for what we call global warming. Carbon monoxide causes temperature inversions, in which a fog of pollution covers an area so that the appropriate mix of oxygen is not allowed. The fog causes an array of breathing disorders that has caused death in some people who had respiratory problems. Waste emissions are taken up into the air, and the weather patterns move it to the polar ice caps where it is frozen harmlessly, keeping the rest of the planet from danger. The temperature inversions would be responsible for melting the polar ice caps, and the toxic waste imbedded in them would be released into the oceans, affecting the marine wildlife.

Carbon monoxide is known to cause temperature inversions that raise the temperature of a city under a foggy globe deprived of oxygen. Many industrial cities in the world have this problem. It can be agreed that mankind is certainly responsible to control waste emissions from artificial automation (Campbell, Reece, and Simon. "Essential Biology." pp. 90-98, 115, 447, 448; c. 2007).

Plants, as a result of photosynthesis, exhale oxygen and inhale carbon dioxide. Mammals inhale oxygen and exhale carbon dioxide. They are even exchanges. These processes cannot be stopped short of death. They are natural processes that are responsible for the life cycles on earth. Since carbon dioxide is a natural part of cyclical life patterns, then it cannot, as a rule, be the problem. It is as necessary as oxygen.

Mikhail Gorbachev said, "Cosmos is my God. Nature is my God (Charlie Rose Show; Oct 23, 1996)." We should not worship the cosmos, but we should know and worship God. We should take the time to know God, because He will tell us what we need to know if we respect Him.

The cosmos, the Laws of Nature, the Earth, planets, stars, and the sun are all objects that have no mind, feelings, emotions, or a body. They do not think for themselves. They are controlled by God like a car is controlled by the person driving it.

How foolish is it, then, to worship "the Cosmos?" It is clear why God commanded us to worship Him and not created things (Exodus 20:3-6).

Governments in the international community have taken scientists seriously on what they have said about carbon dioxide, and have gone so far as to put flatulation sacks on livestock with emissions gauges. If carbon dioxide is found to be above the standard, a farmer is penalized with a tax. This is ridiculous. Emissions standards are for cars, trucks, and industrial complexes, not for animals and humans.

The point is that the initiative to prevent global warming is a special interest group that created an elite group of scientists that "know better" than the rest of the people. They hoped that people would believe them because of their status, education, influence, and power. Al Gore tried to "educate" people that mammals (humans in particular), were the cause for global warming. The study was found to be a ruse. The Commission on Global Warming should not be funded by taxpayer money.

The Homosexual Lobby: The Fabled Gay Gene

When I see studies like, "Is There a 'Gay Gene'? New Genetic Regions Associated With Male Sexual Orientation Found," on www.webmd.com, dated January 5, 2005, citing Dr. Brian Mustanski, Ph. D., who has been receiving grant money to research it, I do not trust it.

In science, it is absolutely imperative that doctors and researchers are impartial about their findings. Therefore, it is important that they are:

1) Not emotionally involved with the subject of their research,

2) Accountable to others for their findings,

3) Not biased toward one view or the other concerning their research, and

4) They cannot be a part of the subject group that they are studying.

Though it is not specified in any of the research that I found on this psychologist, it is obvious that he is a gay man. This alone would disqualify him as an authoritative figure on a gay gene, since he has a partial interest in its results, and a reason to not trust the study. It should be noted, however, that he states that there is "no one gay gene." It cannot be isolated, and it cannot be concluded as to whether a gay gene is passed from the father or the mother to their children. It can, however, be concluded, that homosexual behavior is influenced by the environment. Since homosexuality is not a natural choice to make, it takes a "push." This push usually ends in child molestation, incest, or rape by a trusted family member, friend, or association. No one is "born gay."

According to "Comparing the Lifestyles of Homosexual Couples to Married Couples," an article written by Timothy J. Dailey, Ph. D., at http://www.frc.org/ , homosexuals have multiple partners and only last less than six months at a time. The article states that those homosexuals that lived in monogamous relationships were more likely to contract STDs and AIDS than those who changed partners frequently. Moreover, a majority of homosexuals who considered themselves to be in committed relationships had multiple sex partners outside the relationship. In comparison, married heterosexual couples from the first day they get married remain together a minimum of five years: STDs and AIDS are virtually non-existent. According to the report, fidelity among homosexuals is less than 5%, while fidelity in heterosexual marriages is an average of 80% between males and females. The study concludes that homosexuals do not wish to raise children, while a few with children from previous heterosexual relationships live with their same-sex partners. They are not capable of providing a stable environment for children.

Fairly recently, according to Susan Donaldson of ABC News, on www.abc.go.com in an article, "More Gay Men Choose Surrogacy to Have Children," some older male couples between 40 and 60 who did not want to raise children changed their minds, and adoption was not an option. In the article dated March 12, 2008, Gucci designer Tom Ford, and photographer Richard Buckley did not want children in their 20's, later expressed the desire to hire a host surrogate woman utilizing the sperm of either one or the other. This would allow them to have "their own child" while still engaged in a homosexual relationship. It is not only morally wrong to have a homosexual relationship to begin with, but to hire an outsider to bear a child is preposterous, particularly since both males, certainly capable of making women pregnant, have rejected the idea of normal heterosexual marriage and child-bearing. Furthermore, I am persuaded that it is much more than just a desire to have children. It is a homosexual political agenda to gain a majority consensus through the immoral teaching of children, then teaching them that "they were just BORN that way." It is insane and diabolical to go to such lengths to make an unacceptable behavior acceptable. Homosexuality is against the natural order. It is evident that men need women and vice-versa to have children. God knew what he was doing when he told Adam and Eve to "multiply and replenish the earth." Furthermore, they also had the example in Creation before them, that all things have a male and female component, including plants and trees, earth and seed. Males and females of any species of life on the planet produce after its own kind (Genesis 1:24 - 28). Take notice that God was speaking only to Adam and Eve, the first and only two living humans on earth, male and female. This point over the years had been made clear, and it is evident in our daily lives. The safest sex that any two human beings can have is a male and a female in a committed, loving, and lifelong relationship. Yet, homosexuals continue to defy logic, and continue to prove Paul the Apostle correct in his statement, "For the wages of sin is death; . . . (Romans 6:23a).

For graphical statistics from an authoritative study done by the Family Research Council, see Appendix F.

The Removal of Religious Symbols and Icons of Faith: The destruction of a heritage

In military strategy, if it is desired to conquer a nation, it becomes necessary to

1. **infiltrate,**
2. **permeate,**
3. **eliminate "undesirable" variables,**
4. **remove personal identity,**
5. **remove national identity, and**
6. **Ethnic cleansing (murder, abortion),** and
7. **Replace it with the identity of the conquering nation.**

To infiltrate means to become a part of the nation by means of entrance, working, being friendly, and then perhaps moving into politics to push a specific point of view. If people are being infiltrated, they are actually finding out as much about their subjects as possible in order to find strengths and weaknesses. Then, the infiltrator, attacks the weaknesses. Once the subject is under control, the spy then reports the condition to his fellow spies, and then, however many there are, they begin to permeate society with their beliefs and doctrines such as socialism, communism, or fundamentalist Islam. Each of his companions have pulled a string to their "host" friends, or perhaps found an embarrassing or incriminating piece of propaganda to use. When it is time, then these spies, these new friends from abroad, begin eliminating specific doctrines, ideologies, and doctrines as a threat through gossip, bribery, blackmail, or even "accidental" death. Once the threats are dealt with or eliminated, these "friends" begin to remove individual identities, which will eventually be the removal of the national identity. For instance, you have a cross that you like to wear. It is a symbol of your faith in Jesus Christ. You go everywhere with it, and occasionally, you might wear cufflinks that are shaped like crosses. It didn't seem to bother your friend a few weeks ago, but now he's embarrassed to be seen with you when you wear that cross. This is the beginning of the removal of your identity − if he can get you to willfully remove the cross because it offends him, then he was successful in the beginning of changing your identity. A cross is important to you, but you also like the guy's friendship. So, you remove it. And, you look around, one day, a few weeks later, and all your Christian friends have removed their crosses, as well, and they are hanging around people who are telling them similar things: that it offends them. A couple of months later, you took the cross out of the droor, and put it back around your neck, and your "friend" mocks you, jeers at you, and insists that you remove it. He and his friends have nearly removed your personal identity, one person at a time. You refuse, and what happens next?

If you refuse to change your identity, then, those who used to be your friends that you hung out with, went to church with, worked with, partied with, and grew up with may have already changed their identities. If you wear the cross, and they make fun of you, then they have been successfully brainwashed by their new "friends." You are no longer a part of the group. Then, you go to church, and find that 2000 people have been parted out to cliques. You may have retained your identity, but keep in mind that they have lost theirs. This could take a short span of a few weeks or months, or it could take 5 to 100 years. The infiltrating nation sponsors families that represent its interests, and sends them to the nation to be conquered to raise families and make a way of life, but not according to the nation they live in: it will be according to the nation they came FROM. So, today's children would not believe the same things that yesterday's children did. You have become 80 years old, and have woken up to your house being vandalized, your car windows being broken, and your yard trashed. This is not something you would have done growing up, and it isn't something any of your friends would have done. This is a symptom of the infiltrating nation raising their kids under a different set of ideals.

The children were raised eliminating the ideals of the nation they live in, thus eliminating national identity. They are, plainly, from your city, your state, your country, but they act as if they come from another. This is how you know, that at least around your area, the nation is conquered. An example: "Reverend" Louis Farrakhan and "Reverend" Al Sharpton are preaching something called "social justice." It is, in effect, revenge on our forefathers for slavery, though our legislative system legally repaired the breach, Constitutionally. Therefore, the message of these men is NOT desegregation, peace, and people of all colors walking down the street together. It is NOT of a black man and a white woman marrying and having children together. It is NOT of inter-racial children attending school together. Prior to Malcolm X changing the ideal he was taught by actually visiting Mecca in 1964, having his eyes opened, he preached segregation, separate education, and social justice. After his visit to Mecca, he understood, at that time, that Islam was of all nations, races, and colors. And they lived in peace. When he returned to the United States, his message began to change, and that is when he was assassinated. After his pilgrimage, he believed that Islam was a religion of peace and unity, and rather than using Islam for the purposes of segregation, he uttered his desire to use it for the purposes of unity. He had determined that "whitey" was not the enemy, but rather, racism. I firmly believe that if Malcolm X had lived, he and Dr. Martin Luther King Jr. would've become a powerful team that may have shaped the United States in the "I Have a Dream" speech that MLK Jr. gave. However, shortly thereafter, in 1968, MLK Jr. was assassinated. From federal archives at http://www.archives.gov/press/exhibits/dream-speech.pdf, I have included the original speech of Martin Luther King Junior in Appendix H.

FINAL THOUGHTS FROM THE AUTHOR

Today, the message of the gospel in the Bible about Jesus dying on the cross to save us from our sins to unite us with God, and thus uniting us with one another, has been changed to the message of "social justice." The enemy is HERE, and has nearly removed our identity as a Christian nation, and will soon remove our identity as Americans. If that happens, we will no longer be the richest and most prosperous nation on earth. We will no longer be the most innovative and educated. We will no longer be the first in military technology. We will, in effect, become indebted to the United Nations and the richest of nations over in the Middle East and the Orient. Already, American businesses are being sold to foreign entities, mainly Japan and China. How much longer before we will be waving another banner over our nation? How much longer before we are waging a war of the nations within the United States because we forfeited our national identity? HOW LONG? And, look people, I'm powerless to do anything but write it as it happens, as I've been doing since 2007. YOU have the power. Don't you like being Americans? If YOU don't start fighting soon – there won't be anything left to fight for, as you kneel down, putting your head on the chopping block waiting for the guillotine to fall. Or, watching as mothers have their babies and "doctors" cut their heads off and throw the babies away, much like they do, today. Abortion and ethnic cleansing started in 1972, and generations W, X, Y, and Z have all been raised to believe that the Bible is a fairy tale, and that God is a figment of our imagination. God has been whittled down to the likes of Santa Claus or the Tooth Fairy. Here we are in Generation Z. They don't believe in God, they've accepted some other identity, and they are weak in mind and stature.

Wake up!

Man Cuts Off Wife's Fingers for Studying: Cops

MIGRANT WORKER REPORTEDLY JEALOUS OF HER EDUCATION

By Neal Colgrass, Newser Staff

Posted Dec 17, 2011 1:44 PM CST

(NEWSER) – First he blindfolded his wife and taped her mouth, saying he had surprise present for her. Then he cut off the fingers on her right hand, police say. Rafiqul Islam, 30, a migrant worker in the United Arab Emirates, reportedly confessed after committing the crime in his home country of Bangladesh. "He was enraged," a police chief tells the *Daily Mail*. "He was jealous because while he only had a grade eight standard education, she was off to college to pursue higher studies."

Wife Hawa Akhter, 21, says her husband warned her of "severe consequences" if she didn't abandon her studies. Now she plans to resume studying with her good hand; her fingers were thrown out by her husband and can't be reattached. The alleged attack is only the latest in Bangladesh, a Muslim-majority country where a jobless man recently gouged out his wife's eyes because she pursued a higher education.

British Court Finds Muslim Father Guilty of Murdering Daughter in 'Honor Killing'

Published June 11, 2007

Associated Press

Mahmod Mahmod, 52, was found guilty of murdering his daughter Banaz in 'honor killing.'

A father who ordered his daughter brutally slain for falling in love with the wrong man in a so-called "honor killing" was found guilty of murder on Monday.

Banaz Mahmod➡, 20, was strangled with a boot lace, stuffed into a suitcase and buried in a back garden.

Her death is the latest in an increasing trend of such killings in Britain, home to some 1.8 million Muslims. More than 100 homicides are under investigation as potential "honor killings."

Mahmod Mahmod➡, 52, and his brother **Ari Mahmod**➡, 51, planned the killing during a family meeting, prosecutors told the court. Two others have pleaded guilty in the case. Two more suspects have fled the country. Sentencing is expected later this month.

The men accused the young woman of shaming her family by ending an abusive arranged marriage, becoming too Westernized and falling in love with a man who didn't come from their Iraqi village. The Kurdish family came to Britain in 1998 when Banaz Mahmod was 11.

"She was my present, my future, my hope," said Rahmat Suleimani, 29, Banaz Mahmod's boyfriend.

During the three-month trial, prosecutors said Mahmod's father beat his daughter for using hairspray and adopting other Western ways. Her uncle once told her she would have been "turned to ashes" if she were his daughter and had shamed the family by becoming involved with the Iranian Kurd, her sister 22-year-old Bekhal Mahmod testified.

Banaz Mahmod ran away from home when she was a teenager but returned when her father sent her an audio tape in which he warned he would kill her sisters, her mother and himself if she did not come home, her sister said.

She was later hospitalized after her brother attacked her, the sister told the court. The brother said he had been paid by their father to finish her off but in the end was unable to do it, said the sister, who testified in a full black burqa. She said she still feared for her own life.

The years of Banaz Mahmod's abuse were compounded by police officers who repeatedly dismissed her cries for help.

She first went to police in December 2005, saying she suspected her uncle was trying to kill her and her boyfriend. She sent police a letter naming the men who she thought would later kill her.

On New Year's Eve, she was lured by her father to her grandmother's home, where she suspected he planned to attack her after he forced her to gulp down brandy and approached her while wearing gloves. She escaped by breaking a window and was treated at a hospital.

Police dismissed her suspicions, and one officer, who is under investigation, considered charging her with damages for breaking her grandmother's window.

Laying in her hospital bed after the escape, Mahmod recorded a dramatic video message saying she was "really scared."

The videotape, taken by her boyfriend at the hospital, was shown to the jury during the trial.

After she was released from the hospital, she returned home and tried to convince her family she had stopped seeing her boyfriend.

But friends told the family they spotted the couple together on Jan. 22, 2006.

Soon after, a group of men allegedly approached her boyfriend and tried to lure him into a car but he refused. It was that event that prompted Banaz Mahmod to go to police again. This time officers tried to persuade her to stay in a safe house. She refused, believing that her mother would protect her.

But her mother and father left her alone in the house the next day. Her boyfriend alerted police after time passed in which she failed to send him text messages.

Her body wasn't discovered until three months later after police tracked phone records.

Britain has seen more than 25 women killed by their Muslim relatives in the past decade for offenses they believed brought shame on the family. More than 100 other homicides are under investigation as potential honor killings.

Some Muslim communities in Britain practice Sharia, or strict Islamic law.

"We're seeing an increase around the world, due in part to the rise in Islamic fundamentalism," said Diana Nammi with the London-based **Iranian and Kurdish Women's Rights Organization**⊟➔.

APPENDIX B

Excerpts of Sharia Law (http://www.al-islam.org/laws/)

84. * The following ten things are essentially najis (unclean):

- ☐ Urine
- ☐ Faeces
- ☐ Semen
- ☐ Dead body
- ☐ Blood
- ☐ Dog
- ☐ Pig
- ☐ Kafir
- ☐ Alcoholic liquors
- ☐ The sweat of an animal who persistently eats najasat (Dead bodies).

Kafir (unbeliever)

107. * An infidel i.e. a person who does not believe in Allah and His Oneness, is najis. Similarly, Ghulat who believe in any of the holy twelve Imams as God, or that they are incarnations of God, and Khawarij and Nawasib who express enmity towards the holy Imams, are also najis. And similar is the case of those who deny Prophethood, or any of the necessary laws of Islam, like, namaz and fasting, which are believed by the Muslims as a part of Islam, and which they also know as such.

As regards the people of the Book (i.e. the Jews and the Christians) who do not accept the Prophethood of Prophet Muhammad bin Abdullah (Peace be upon him and his progeny), they are commonly considered najis, but it is not improbable that they are Pak (ritually pure). However, it is better to avoid them.

108. The entire body of a Kafir, including his hair and nails, and all liquid substances of his body, are najis.

109. * If the parents, paternal grandmother and paternal grandfather of a minor child are all kafir, that child is najis, except when he is intelligent enough, and professes Islam. When, even one person from his parents or grandparents is a Muslim, the child is Pak (The details will be explained in rule 217).

110. * A person about whom it is not known whether he is a Muslim or not, and if no signs exist to establish him as a Muslim, he will be considered Pak. But he will not have the privileges of a Muslim, like, he cannot marry a Muslim woman, nor can he be buried in a Muslim cemetery.

111. Any person who abuses any of the twelve holy Imams on account of enmity, is najis.

1. 217. * The child of an unbeliever becomes Pak by Taba'iyat, in two cases:

    1. If an unbeliever embraces Islam, his child in subjection to him becomes Pak. Similarly, if the mother, paternal grandfather, or paternal grandmother of a child embraces Islam, the child will become Pak, provided that it is in their custody and care.

    2. If the child of an unbeliever is captured by Muslims, and his father, paternal grandfather or maternal grandfather is not with him, he becomes Pak. In both the cases, the child becomes Pak by subjection, on the condition that if it has attained the age of understanding and discerning, it does not show inclination to Kufr. A kafir is in the category of unclean. That means, basically, that Jews and all those who live in the west and uphold the principles of the Constitution such as the freedom of speech, the freedom of religion, and the right to reject religion or philosophy are the enemy. In the United States, we embrace differing points of view, learn from each other's philosophies and religions, and our culture is enhanced by it. There are no violent demonstrations, shootings, or beheadings over an atheist monument that was displayed next to the Ten

Commandments
(http://www.foxnews.com/us/2013/06/30/atheists-unveil-monument-by-ten-commandments/).

As shown by recent history in Appendix A, Islam stifles growth and the acquisition of knowledge outside Islam, and kills those who oppose it.

The following excerpts are somewhat an antithesis to conventional moral law and the Torah; therefore, I caution you: it pertains to marriage, sex, and incestual relationships.

Rules regarding temporary marriage, incest, and fornication; Sharia Law:

2401. A man cannot marry the niece (brother's or sister's daughter) of his wife without her permission. But if he marries his nieces without his wife's permission, and she later consents to the marriage, it will be in order.

2402. * If the wife learns that her husband has married her niece (brother's daughter or sister's daughter) and keeps quiet, and if she later consents to that marriage, it will be in order. If she does not consent later, the marriage will be void.

2403. * If before marrying his maternal or paternal aunt's daughter, a person commits incest (sexual intercourse) with her mother, he cannot marry that girl on the basis of precaution.

2404. * If a person marries his paternal or maternal aunt's daughter, and after having consummated the marriage, commits incest with her mother, this act will not become the cause of their separation. And the same rule applies if he commits incest with her mother after the Nikah, but before having consummated the marriage with her, although the recommended precaution is that in this circumstance he should separate from her by giving her divorce.

2405. * If a person commits fornication with a woman other than his paternal or maternal aunt, the recommended precaution is that he should not marry her daughter. In fact, if he marries a woman, and commits fornication with her mother before having sexual intercourse with her, the recommended precaution is that he should separate from her, but if he has sexual intercourse with her, and thereafter commits fornication with her mother, it is not necessary for him to get separated from her.

2406. * A Muslim woman cannot marry a non-Muslim, and a male Muslim also cannot marry a non-Muslim woman who are not Ahlul Kitab.

However, there is no harm in contracting temporary marriage with Jewish and Christian women, but the obligatory precaution is that a Muslim should not take them in permanent marriage. There are certain sects like Khawarij, Ghulat and Nawasib who claim to be Muslims, but are classified as non-Muslims. Muslim men and women cannot contract permanent or temporary marriage with them.

Traditional Judeo-Christian morality in the Old Testament makes it clear: grandparents, parents, sisters, brothers, aunts, uncles, nieces, nephews, in-laws, same sex, and animals are clearly off limits to sexual contact of any kind.

Leviticus 18:1-30

Authorized (King James) Version (AKJV)

18 And the LORD spake unto Moses, saying, [2] Speak unto the children of Israel, and say unto them, I am the LORD your God. [3] After the doings of the land of Egypt, wherein ye dwelt, shall ye not do: and after the doings of the land of Canaan, whither I bring you, shall ye not do: neither shall ye walk in their ordinances. [4] Ye shall do my judgments, and keep mine ordinances, to walk therein: I *am* the LORD your God. [5] Ye shall therefore keep my statutes, and my judgments: which if a man do, he shall live in them: I *am* the LORD.

[6] None of you shall approach to any that is near of kin to him, to uncover *their* nakedness: I *am* the LORD. [7] The nakedness of thy father, or the nakedness of thy mother, shalt thou not uncover: she *is* thy mother; thou shalt not uncover her nakedness. [8] The nakedness of thy father's wife shalt thou not uncover: it *is* thy father's nakedness. [9] The nakedness of thy sister, the daughter of thy father, or daughter of thy mother, *whether she be* born at home, or born abroad, *even* their nakedness thou shalt not uncover. [10] The nakedness of thy son's daughter, or of thy daughter's daughter, *even* their nakedness thou shalt not uncover: for theirs *is* thine own nakedness. [11] The nakedness of thy father's wife's daughter, begotten of thy father, she *is* thy sister, thou shalt not uncover her nakedness. [12] Thou shalt not uncover the nakedness of thy father's sister: she *is* thy father's near kinswoman. [13] Thou shalt not uncover the nakedness of thy mother's sister: for she *is* thy mother's near kinswoman. [14] Thou shalt not uncover the nakedness of thy father's brother, thou shalt not approach to his wife: she *is* thine aunt. [15] Thou shalt not uncover the nakedness of thy daughter in law: she *is* thy son's wife; thou shalt not uncover her

nakedness. [16] Thou shalt not uncover the nakedness of thy brother's wife: it *is* thy brother's nakedness. [17] Thou shalt not uncover the nakedness of a woman and her daughter, neither shalt thou take her son's daughter, or her daughter's daughter, to uncover her nakedness; *for* they *are* her near kinswomen: it *is* wickedness. [18] Neither shalt thou take a wife to her sister, to vex *her*, to uncover her nakedness, beside the other in her life *time*. [19] Also thou shalt not approach unto a woman to uncover her nakedness, as long as she is put apart for her uncleanness. [20] Moreover thou shalt not lie carnally with thy neighbour's wife, to defile thyself with her. [21] And thou shalt not let any of thy seed pass through *the fire* to Molech, neither shalt thou profane the name of thy God: I *am* the LORD. [22] Thou shalt not lie with mankind, as with womankind: it *is* abomination. [23] Neither shalt thou lie with any beast to defile thyself therewith: neither shall any woman stand before a beast to lie down thereto: it *is* confusion.

[24] Defile not ye yourselves in any of these things: for in all these the nations are defiled which I cast out before you: [25] and the land is defiled: therefore I do visit the iniquity thereof upon it, and the land itself vomiteth out her inhabitants. [26] Ye shall therefore keep my statutes and my judgments, and shall not commit *any* of these abominations; *neither* any of your own nation, nor any stranger that sojourneth among you: [27] (for all these abominations have the men of the land done, which *were* before you, and the land is defiled;) [28] that the land spue not you out also, when ye defile it, as it spued out the nations that *were* before you. [29] For whosoever shall commit any of these abominations, even the souls that commit *them* shall be cut off from among their people. [30] Therefore shall ye keep mine ordinance, that *ye* commit not *any one* of these abominable customs, which were committed before you, and that ye defile not yourselves therein: I *am* the LORD your God.

The Lord told Moses that these were sins not to be committed, or the very land will refuse to yield its fruit, and eject the occupants. And there is no "temporary" marriage in the Bible. Either you are or you aren't. Ideally, marriage other than certain violations, is a life-long commitment sealed by God (NOT Allah).

Here is an interesting fact: Since Christianity is based on the Bible, written by Jews, then it is only logical that we should also base meanings of words from the Old Testament on the Hebrew language. The Hebrew word, "הלא, alah," used in Numbers 5:21 does not mean "God." It means, "curse." It is usually attributed to the

unfaithfulness of a woman
(http://prophesite.wordpress.com/2012/02/01/allah-means-
curse-in-hebrew-more-than-a-coincidence/).

APPENDIX C

Declaration of Independence

(Adopted by Congress on July 4, 1776)

The Unanimous Declaration
of the Thirteen United States of America

When, in the course of human events, it becomes necessary for
one people to dissolve the political bands which have connected
them with another, and to assume among the powers of the earth,
the separate and equal station to which the laws of nature and of
nature's God entitle them, a decent respect to the opinions of
mankind requires that they should declare the causes which impel
them to the separation.

We hold these truths to be self-evident, that all men are created
equal, that they are endowed by their Creator with certain
unalienable rights, that among these are life, liberty and the
pursuit of happiness. That to secure these rights, governments are
instituted among men, deriving their just powers from the consent
of the governed. That whenever any form of government becomes
destructive to these ends, it is the right of the people to alter or to
abolish it, and to institute new government, laying its foundation
on such principles and organizing its powers in such form, as to
them shall seem most likely to effect their safety and happiness.
Prudence, indeed, will dictate that governments long established
should not be changed for light and transient causes; and
accordingly all experience hath shown that mankind are more
disposed to suffer, while evils are sufferable, than to right
themselves by abolishing the forms to which they are accustomed.
But when a long train of abuses and usurpations, pursuing
invariably the same object evinces a design to reduce them under
absolute despotism, it is their right, it is their duty, to throw off
such government, and to provide new guards for their future
security. --Such has been the patient sufferance of these colonies;

and such is now the necessity which constrains them to alter their former systems of government. The history of the present King of Great Britain is a history of repeated injuries and usurpations, all having in direct object the establishment of an absolute tyranny over these states. To prove this, let facts be submitted to a candid world.

He has refused his assent to laws, the most wholesome and necessary for the public good.

He has forbidden his governors to pass laws of immediate and pressing importance, unless suspended in their operation till his assent should be obtained; and when so suspended, he has utterly neglected to attend to them.

He has refused to pass other laws for the accommodation of large districts of people, unless those people would relinquish the right of representation in the legislature, a right inestimable to them and formidable to tyrants only.

He has called together legislative bodies at places unusual, uncomfortable, and distant from the depository of their public records, for the sole purpose of fatiguing them into compliance with his measures.

He has dissolved representative houses repeatedly, for opposing with manly firmness his invasions on the rights of the people.

He has refused for a long time, after such dissolutions, to cause others to be elected; whereby the legislative powers, incapable of annihilation, have returned to the people at large for their exercise; the state remaining in the meantime exposed to all the dangers of invasion from without, and convulsions within.

He has endeavored to prevent the population of these states; for that purpose obstructing the laws for naturalization of foreigners; refusing to pass others to encourage their migration hither, and raising the conditions of new appropriations of lands.

He has obstructed the administration of justice, by refusing his assent to laws for establishing judiciary powers.

He has made judges dependent on his will alone, for the tenure of their offices, and the amount and payment of their salaries.

He has erected a multitude of new offices, and sent hither swarms of officers to harass our people, and eat out their substance.

He has kept among us, in times of peace, standing armies without the consent of our legislature.

He has affected to render the military independent of and superior to civil power.

He has combined with others to subject us to a jurisdiction foreign to our constitution, and unacknowledged by our laws; giving his assent to their acts of pretended legislation:

For quartering large bodies of armed troops among us:

For protecting them, by mock trial, from punishment for any murders which they should commit on the inhabitants of these states:

For cutting off our trade with all parts of the world:

For imposing taxes on us without our consent:

For depriving us in many cases, of the benefits of trial by jury:

For transporting us beyond seas to be tried for pretended offenses:

For abolishing the free system of English laws in a neighboring province, establishing therein an arbitrary government, and enlarging its boundaries so as to render it at once an example and fit instrument for introducing the same absolute rule in these colonies:

For taking away our charters, abolishing our most valuable laws, and altering fundamentally the forms of our governments:

For suspending our own legislatures, and declaring themselves invested with power to legislate for us in all cases whatsoever.

He has abdicated government here, by declaring us out of his protection and waging war against us.

He has plundered our seas, ravaged our coasts, burned our towns, and destroyed the lives of our people.

He is at this time transporting large armies of foreign mercenaries to complete the works of death, desolation and tyranny, already begun with circumstances of cruelty and perfidy scarcely paralleled in the most barbarous ages, and totally unworthy the head of a civilized nation.

He has constrained our fellow citizens taken captive on the high seas to bear arms against their country, to become the executioners of their friends and brethren, or to fall themselves by their hands.

He has excited domestic insurrections amongst us, and has endeavored to bring on the inhabitants of our frontiers, the merciless Indian savages, whose known rule of warfare, is undistinguished destruction of all ages, sexes and conditions.

In every stage of these oppressions we have petitioned for redress in the most humble terms: our repeated petitions have been answered only by repeated injury. A prince, whose character is thus marked by every act which may define a tyrant, is unfit to be the ruler of a free people.

Nor have we been wanting in attention to our British brethren. We have warned them from time to time of attempts by their legislature to extend an unwarrantable jurisdiction over us. We have reminded them of the circumstances of our emigration and settlement here. We have appealed to their native justice and magnanimity, and we have conjured them by the ties of our common kindred to disavow these usurpations, which, would inevitably interrupt our connections and correspondence. They too have been deaf to the voice of justice and of consanguinity. We must, therefore, acquiesce in the necessity, which denounces our separation, and hold them, as we hold the rest of mankind, enemies in war, in peace friends.

We, therefore, the representatives of the United States of America, in General Congress, assembled, appealing to the Supreme Judge of the world for the rectitude of our intentions, do, in the name, and by the authority of the good people of these colonies, solemnly publish and declare, that these united colonies are, and of right ought to be free and independent states; that they are absolved from all allegiance to the British Crown, and that all political connection between them and the state of Great Britain, is and ought to be totally dissolved; and that as free and independent states, they have full power to levy war, conclude peace, contract alliances, establish commerce, and to do all other acts and things which independent states may of right do. And for the support of this declaration, with a firm reliance on the protection of Divine Providence, we mutually pledge to each other our lives, our fortunes and our sacred honor.

New Hampshire: Josiah Bartlett, William Whipple, Matthew Thornton

Massachusetts: John Hancock, Samual Adams, John Adams, Robert Treat Paine, Elbridge Gerry

Rhode Island: Stephen Hopkins, William Ellery

Connecticut: Roger Sherman, Samuel Huntington, William Williams, Oliver Wolcott

New York: William Floyd, Philip Livingston, Francis Lewis, Lewis Morris

New Jersey: Richard Stockton, John Witherspoon, Francis Hopkinson, John Hart, Abraham Clark

Pennsylvania: Robert Morris, Benjamin Rush, Benjamin Franklin, John Morton, George Clymer, James Smith, George Taylor, James Wilson, George Ross

Delaware: Caesar Rodney, George Read, Thomas McKean

Maryland: Samuel Chase, William Paca, Thomas Stone, Charles Carroll of Carrollton

Virginia: George Wythe, Richard Henry Lee, Thomas Jefferson, Benjamin Harrison, Thomas Nelson, Jr., Francis Lightfoot Lee, Carter Braxton

North Carolina: William Hooper, Joseph Hewes, John Penn

South Carolina: Edward Rutledge, Thomas Heyward, Jr., Thomas Lynch, Jr., Arthur Middleton

Georgia: Button Gwinnett, Lyman Hall, George Walton

Source: The Pennsylvania Packet, July 8, 1776

APPENDIX D

The Constitution

The Constitution of the United States: A Transcription

Note: *The following text is a transcription of the Constitution in its **original** form.*
Items that are hyperlinked have since been amended or superseded.

We the People of the United States, in Order to form a more perfect Union, establish Justice, insure domestic Tranquility, provide for the common defence, promote the general Welfare, and secure the Blessings of Liberty to ourselves and our Posterity, do ordain and establish this Constitution for the United States of America.

Article. I.

Section. 1.

All legislative Powers herein granted shall be vested in a Congress of the United States, which shall consist of a Senate and House of Representatives.

Section. 2.

The House of Representatives shall be composed of Members chosen every second Year by the People of the several States, and the Electors in each State shall have the Qualifications requisite for Electors of the most numerous Branch of the State Legislature.

No Person shall be a Representative who shall not have attained to the Age of twenty five Years, and been seven Years a Citizen of the United States, and who shall not, when elected, be an Inhabitant of that State in which he shall be chosen.

Representatives and direct Taxes shall be apportioned among the several States which may be included within this Union, according to their respective Numbers, which shall be determined by adding to the whole Number of free Persons, including those bound to Service for a Term of Years, and excluding Indians not taxed, three fifths of all other Persons. The actual Enumeration shall be made within three Years after the first Meeting of the Congress of the United States, and within every subsequent Term of ten Years, in such Manner as they shall by Law direct. The Number of Representatives shall not exceed one for every thirty Thousand, but each State shall have at Least one Representative; and until such enumeration shall be made, the State of New Hampshire shall be entitled to chuse three, Massachusetts eight, Rhode-Island and Providence Plantations one, Connecticut five, New-York six, New Jersey four, Pennsylvania eight, Delaware one, Maryland six, Virginia ten, North Carolina five, South Carolina five, and Georgia three.

When vacancies happen in the Representation from any State, the Executive Authority thereof shall issue Writs of Election to fill such Vacancies.

The House of Representatives shall chuse their Speaker and other Officers; and shall have the sole Power of Impeachment.

Section. 3.

The Senate of the United States shall be composed of two Senators from each State, chosen by the Legislature thereof for six Years; and each Senator shall have one Vote.

Immediately after they shall be assembled in Consequence of the first Election, they shall be divided as equally as may be into three Classes. The Seats of the Senators of the first Class shall be vacated at the Expiration of the second Year, of the second Class at the Expiration of the fourth Year, and of the third Class at the Expiration of the sixth Year, so that one third may be chosen every second Year; and if Vacancies happen by Resignation, or otherwise, during the Recess of the Legislature of any State, the Executive thereof may make temporary Appointments until the next Meeting of the Legislature, which shall then fill such Vacancies.

No Person shall be a Senator who shall not have attained to the Age of thirty Years, and been nine Years a Citizen of the United States, and who shall not, when elected, be an Inhabitant of that State for which he shall be chosen.

The Vice President of the United States shall be President of the Senate, but shall have no Vote, unless they be equally divided.

The Senate shall chuse their other Officers, and also a President pro tempore, in the Absence of the Vice President, or when he shall exercise the Office of President of the United States.

The Senate shall have the sole Power to try all Impeachments. When sitting for that Purpose, they shall be on Oath or Affirmation. When the President of the United States is tried, the Chief Justice shall preside: And no Person shall be convicted without the Concurrence of two thirds of the Members present.

Judgment in Cases of Impeachment shall not extend further than to removal from Office, and disqualification to hold and enjoy any Office of honor, Trust or Profit under the United States: but the Party convicted shall nevertheless be liable and subject to Indictment, Trial, Judgment and Punishment, according to Law.

Section. 4.

The Times, Places and Manner of holding Elections for Senators and Representatives, shall be prescribed in each State by the Legislature thereof; but the Congress may at any time by Law make or alter such Regulations, except as to the Places of chusing Senators.

The Congress shall assemble at least once in every Year, and such Meeting shall be on the first Monday in December, unless they shall by Law appoint a different Day.

Section. 5.

Each House shall be the Judge of the Elections, Returns and Qualifications of its own Members, and a Majority of each shall constitute a Quorum to do Business; but a smaller Number may adjourn from day to day, and may be authorized to compel the Attendance of absent Members, in such Manner, and under such Penalties as each House may provide.

Each House may determine the Rules of its Proceedings, punish its Members for disorderly Behaviour, and, with the Concurrence of two thirds, expel a Member.

Each House shall keep a Journal of its Proceedings, and from time to time publish the same, excepting such Parts as may in their Judgment require Secrecy; and the Yeas and Nays of the Members of either House on any question shall, at the Desire of one fifth of those Present, be entered on the Journal.

Neither House, during the Session of Congress, shall, without the Consent of the other, adjourn for more than three days, nor to any other Place than that in which the two Houses shall be sitting.

Section. 6.

The Senators and Representatives shall receive a Compensation for their Services, to be ascertained by Law, and paid out of the Treasury of the United States. They shall in all Cases, except Treason, Felony and Breach of the Peace, be privileged from Arrest during their Attendance at the Session of their respective Houses, and in going to and returning from the same; and for any Speech or Debate in either House, they shall not be questioned in any other Place.

No Senator or Representative shall, during the Time for which he was elected, be appointed to any civil Office under the Authority of the United States, which shall have been created, or the Emoluments whereof shall have been encreased during such time; and no Person holding any Office under the United States, shall be a Member of either House during his Continuance in Office.

Section. 7.

All Bills for raising Revenue shall originate in the House of Representatives; but the Senate may propose or concur with Amendments as on other Bills.

Every Bill which shall have passed the House of Representatives and the Senate, shall, before it become a Law, be presented to the President of the United States: If he approve he shall sign it, but if not he shall return it, with his Objections to that House in which it shall have originated, who shall enter the Objections at large on their Journal, and proceed to reconsider it. If after such Reconsideration two thirds of that House shall agree to pass the Bill, it shall be sent, together with the Objections, to the other House, by which it shall likewise be reconsidered, and if approved by two thirds of that House, it shall become a Law. But in all such Cases the Votes of both Houses shall be determined by yeas and Nays, and the Names of the Persons voting for and against the Bill shall be entered on the Journal of each House respectively. If any Bill shall not be returned by the President within ten Days (Sundays excepted) after it shall have been presented to him, the Same shall be a Law, in like Manner as if he had signed it, unless the Congress by their Adjournment prevent its Return, in which Case it shall not be a Law.

Every Order, Resolution, or Vote to which the Concurrence of the Senate and House of Representatives may be necessary (except on a question of Adjournment) shall be presented to the President of the United States; and before the Same shall take Effect, shall be approved by him, or being disapproved by him, shall be repassed by two thirds of the Senate and House of Representatives, according to the Rules and Limitations prescribed in the Case of a Bill.

Section. 8.

The Congress shall have Power To lay and collect Taxes, Duties, Imposts and Excises, to pay the Debts and provide for the common Defence and general Welfare of the United States; but all Duties, Imposts and Excises shall be uniform throughout the United States;

To borrow Money on the credit of the United States;

To regulate Commerce with foreign Nations, and among the several States, and with the Indian Tribes;

64

To establish an uniform Rule of Naturalization, and uniform Laws on the subject of Bankruptcies throughout the United States;

To coin Money, regulate the Value thereof, and of foreign Coin, and fix the Standard of Weights and Measures;

To provide for the Punishment of counterfeiting the Securities and current Coin of the United States;

To establish Post Offices and post Roads;

To promote the Progress of Science and useful Arts, by securing for limited Times to Authors and Inventors the exclusive Right to their respective Writings and Discoveries;

To constitute Tribunals inferior to the supreme Court;

To define and punish Piracies and Felonies committed on the high Seas, and Offences against the Law of Nations;

To declare War, grant Letters of Marque and Reprisal, and make Rules concerning Captures on Land and Water;

To raise and support Armies, but no Appropriation of Money to that Use shall be for a longer Term than two Years;

To provide and maintain a Navy;

To make Rules for the Government and Regulation of the land and naval Forces;

To provide for calling forth the Militia to execute the Laws of the Union, suppress Insurrections and repel Invasions;

To provide for organizing, arming, and disciplining, the Militia, and for governing such Part of them as may be employed in the Service of the United States, reserving to the States respectively, the Appointment of the Officers, and the Authority of training the Militia according to the discipline prescribed by Congress;

To exercise exclusive Legislation in all Cases whatsoever, over such District (not exceeding ten Miles square) as may, by Cession of particular States, and the Acceptance of Congress, become the Seat of the Government of the United States, and to exercise like Authority over all Places purchased by the Consent of the Legislature of the State in which the Same shall be, for the Erection of Forts, Magazines, Arsenals, dock-Yards, and other needful Buildings;--And

To make all Laws which shall be necessary and proper for carrying into Execution the foregoing Powers, and all other Powers vested by this Constitution in the Government of the United States, or in any Department or Officer thereof.

Section. 9.

The Migration or Importation of such Persons as any of the States now existing shall think proper to admit, shall not be prohibited by the Congress prior to the Year one thousand eight hundred and eight, but a Tax or duty may be imposed on such Importation, not exceeding ten dollars for each Person.

The Privilege of the Writ of Habeas Corpus shall not be suspended, unless when in Cases of Rebellion or Invasion the public Safety may require it.

No Bill of Attainder or ex post facto Law shall be passed.

No Capitation, or other direct, Tax shall be laid, unless in Proportion to the Census or enumeration herein before directed to be taken.

No Tax or Duty shall be laid on Articles exported from any State.

No Preference shall be given by any Regulation of Commerce or Revenue to the Ports of one State over those of another; nor shall Vessels bound to, or from, one State, be obliged to enter, clear, or pay Duties in another.

No Money shall be drawn from the Treasury, but in Consequence of Appropriations made by Law; and a regular Statement and Account of the Receipts and Expenditures of all public Money shall be published from time to time.

No Title of Nobility shall be granted by the United States: And no Person holding any Office of Profit or Trust under them, shall, without the Consent of the Congress, accept of any present, Emolument, Office, or Title, of any kind whatever, from any King, Prince, or foreign State.

Section. 10.

No State shall enter into any Treaty, Alliance, or Confederation; grant Letters of Marque and Reprisal; coin Money; emit Bills of Credit; make any Thing but gold and silver Coin a Tender in Payment of Debts; pass any Bill of Attainder, ex post facto Law, or Law impairing the Obligation of Contracts, or grant any Title of Nobility.

No State shall, without the Consent of the Congress, lay any Imposts or Duties on Imports or Exports, except what may be absolutely necessary for executing it's inspection Laws: and the net Produce of all Duties and Imposts, laid by any State on Imports or Exports, shall be for the Use of the Treasury of the United States; and all such Laws shall be subject to the Revision and Controul of the Congress.

No State shall, without the Consent of Congress, lay any Duty of Tonnage, keep Troops, or Ships of War in time of Peace, enter into any Agreement or Compact with another State, or with a foreign Power, or engage in War, unless actually invaded, or in such imminent Danger as will not admit of delay.

Article. II.

Section. 1.

The executive Power shall be vested in a President of the United States of America. He shall hold his Office during the Term of four Years, and, together with the Vice President, chosen for the same Term, be elected, as follows:

Each State shall appoint, in such Manner as the Legislature thereof may direct, a Number of Electors, equal to the whole Number of Senators and Representatives to which the State may be entitled in the Congress: but no Senator or Representative, or Person holding an Office of Trust or Profit under the United States, shall be appointed an Elector.

The Electors shall meet in their respective States, and vote by Ballot for two Persons, of whom one at least shall not be an Inhabitant of the same State with themselves. And they shall make a List of all the Persons voted for, and of the Number of Votes for each; which List they shall sign and certify, and transmit sealed to the Seat of the Government of the United States, directed to the President of the Senate. The President of the Senate shall, in the Presence of the Senate and House of Representatives, open all the Certificates, and the Votes shall then be counted. The Person having the greatest Number of Votes shall be the President, if such Number be a Majority of the whole Number of Electors appointed; and if there be more than one who have such Majority, and have an equal Number of Votes, then the House of Representatives shall immediately chuse by Ballot one of them for President; and if no Person have a Majority, then from the five highest on the List the said House shall in like Manner chuse the President. But in chusing the President, the Votes shall be taken by States, the Representation from each State having one Vote; A quorum for this purpose shall consist of a Member or Members from two thirds of the States, and a Majority of all the States shall be necessary to a Choice. In every Case, after the Choice of the President, the Person having the greatest Number of Votes of the Electors shall be the Vice President. But if there should remain two or more who have equal Votes, the Senate shall chuse from them by Ballot the Vice President.

The Congress may determine the Time of chusing the Electors, and the Day on which they shall give their Votes; which Day shall be the same throughout the United States.

No Person except a natural born Citizen, or a Citizen of the United States, at the time of the Adoption of this Constitution, shall be eligible to the Office of President; neither shall any Person be eligible to that Office who shall not have attained to the Age of thirty five Years, and been fourteen Years a Resident within the United States.

In Case of the Removal of the President from Office, or of his Death, Resignation, or Inability to discharge the Powers and Duties of the said Office, the Same shall devolve on the Vice President, and the Congress may by Law provide for the Case of Removal, Death, Resignation or Inability, both of the President and Vice President, declaring what Officer shall then act as President, and such Officer shall act accordingly, until the Disability be removed, or a President shall be elected.

The President shall, at stated Times, receive for his Services, a Compensation, which shall neither be increased nor diminished during the Period for which he shall have been elected, and he shall not receive within that Period any other Emolument from the United States, or any of them.

Before he enter on the Execution of his Office, he shall take the following Oath or Affirmation:--"I do solemnly swear (or affirm) that I will faithfully execute the Office of President of the United States, and will to the best of my Ability, preserve, protect and defend the Constitution of the United States."

Section. 2.

The President shall be Commander in Chief of the Army and Navy of the United States, and of the Militia of the several States, when called into the actual Service of the United States; he may require the Opinion, in writing, of the principal Officer in each of the executive Departments, upon any Subject relating to the Duties of their respective Offices, and he shall have Power to grant Reprieves and Pardons for Offences against the United States, except in Cases of Impeachment.

He shall have Power, by and with the Advice and Consent of the Senate, to make Treaties, provided two thirds of the Senators present concur; and he shall nominate, and by and with the Advice and Consent of the Senate, shall appoint Ambassadors, other public Ministers and Consuls, Judges of the supreme Court, and all other Officers of the United States, whose Appointments are not herein otherwise provided for, and which shall be established by Law: but the Congress may by Law vest the Appointment of such inferior Officers, as they think proper, in the President alone, in the Courts of Law, or in the Heads of Departments.

The President shall have Power to fill up all Vacancies that may happen during the Recess of the Senate, by granting Commissions which shall expire at the End of their next Session.

Section. 3.

He shall from time to time give to the Congress Information of the State of the Union, and recommend to their Consideration such Measures as he shall judge necessary and expedient; he may, on extraordinary Occasions, convene both Houses, or either of them, and in Case of Disagreement between them, with Respect to the Time of Adjournment, he may adjourn them to such Time as he shall think proper; he shall receive Ambassadors and other public Ministers; he shall take Care that the Laws be faithfully executed, and shall Commission all the Officers of the United States.

Section. 4.

The President, Vice President and all civil Officers of the United States, shall be removed from Office on Impeachment for, and Conviction of, Treason, Bribery, or other high Crimes and Misdemeanors.

Article III.

Section. 1.

The judicial Power of the United States shall be vested in one supreme Court, and in such inferior Courts as the Congress may from time to time ordain and establish. The Judges, both of the supreme and inferior Courts, shall hold their Offices during good Behaviour, and shall, at stated Times, receive for their Services a Compensation, which shall not be diminished during their Continuance in Office.

Section. 2.

The judicial Power shall extend to all Cases, in Law and Equity, arising under this Constitution, the Laws of the United States, and Treaties made, or which shall be made, under their Authority;--to all Cases affecting Ambassadors, other public Ministers and Consuls;--to all Cases of admiralty and maritime Jurisdiction;--to Controversies to which the United States shall be a Party;--to Controversies between two or more States;-- between a State and Citizens of another State,--between Citizens of different States,-- between Citizens of the same State claiming Lands under Grants of different States, and between a State, or the Citizens thereof, and foreign States, Citizens or Subjects.

In all Cases affecting Ambassadors, other public Ministers and Consuls, and those in which a State shall be Party, the supreme Court shall have original Jurisdiction. In all the other Cases before mentioned, the supreme Court shall have appellate Jurisdiction, both as to Law and Fact, with such Exceptions, and under such Regulations as the Congress shall make.

The Trial of all Crimes, except in Cases of Impeachment, shall be by Jury; and such Trial shall be held in the State where the said Crimes shall have been committed; but when not committed within any State, the Trial shall be at such Place or Places as the Congress may by Law have directed.

Section. 3.

Treason against the United States, shall consist only in levying War against them, or in adhering to their Enemies, giving them Aid and Comfort. No Person shall be convicted of Treason unless on the Testimony of two Witnesses to the same overt Act, or on Confession in open Court.

The Congress shall have Power to declare the Punishment of Treason, but no Attainder of Treason shall work Corruption of Blood, or Forfeiture except during the Life of the Person attainted.

Article. IV.

Section. 1.

Full Faith and Credit shall be given in each State to the public Acts, Records, and judicial Proceedings of every other State. And the Congress may by general Laws prescribe the Manner in which such Acts, Records and Proceedings shall be proved, and the Effect thereof.

Section. 2.

The Citizens of each State shall be entitled to all Privileges and Immunities of Citizens in the several States.

A Person charged in any State with Treason, Felony, or other Crime, who shall flee from Justice, and be found in another State, shall on Demand of the executive Authority of the State from which he fled, be delivered up, to be removed to the State having Jurisdiction of the Crime.

No Person held to Service or Labour in one State, under the Laws thereof, escaping into another, shall, in Consequence of any Law or Regulation therein, be discharged from such Service or Labour, but shall be delivered up on Claim of the Party to whom such Service or Labour may be due.

Section. 3.

New States may be admitted by the Congress into this Union; but no new State shall be formed or erected within the Jurisdiction of any other State; nor any State be formed by the Junction of two or more States, or Parts of States, without the Consent of the Legislatures of the States concerned as well as of the Congress.

The Congress shall have Power to dispose of and make all needful Rules and Regulations respecting the Territory or other Property belonging to the United States; and nothing in this Constitution shall be so construed as to Prejudice any Claims of the United States, or of any particular State.

Section. 4.

The United States shall guarantee to every State in this Union a Republican Form of Government, and shall protect each of them against Invasion; and on Application of the Legislature, or of the Executive (when the Legislature cannot be convened), against domestic Violence.

Article. V.

The Congress, whenever two thirds of both Houses shall deem it necessary, shall propose Amendments to this Constitution, or, on the Application of the Legislatures of two thirds of the several States, shall call a Convention for proposing Amendments, which, in either Case, shall be valid to all Intents and Purposes, as Part of this Constitution, when ratified by the Legislatures of three fourths of the several States, or by Conventions in three fourths thereof, as the one or the other Mode of Ratification may be proposed by the Congress; Provided that no Amendment which may be made prior to the Year One thousand eight hundred and eight shall in any Manner affect the first and fourth Clauses in the Ninth Section of the first Article; and that no State, without its Consent, shall be deprived of its equal Suffrage in the Senate.

Article. VI.

All Debts contracted and Engagements entered into, before the Adoption of this Constitution, shall be as valid against the United States under this Constitution, as under the Confederation.

This Constitution, and the Laws of the United States which shall be made in Pursuance thereof; and all Treaties made, or which shall be made, under the Authority of the United States, shall be the supreme Law of the Land; and the Judges in every State shall be bound thereby, any Thing in the Constitution or Laws of any State to the Contrary notwithstanding.

The Senators and Representatives before mentioned, and the Members of the several State Legislatures, and all executive and judicial Officers, both of the United States and of the several States, shall be bound by Oath or Affirmation, to support this Constitution; but no religious Test shall ever be required as a Qualification to any Office or public Trust under the United States.

Article. VII.

The Ratification of the Conventions of nine States, shall be sufficient for the Establishment of this Constitution between the States so ratifying the Same.

The Word, "the," being interlined between the seventh and eighth Lines of the first Page, the Word "Thirty" being partly written on an Erazure in the fifteenth Line of the first Page, The Words "is tried" being interlined between the thirty second and thirty third Lines of the first Page and the Word "the" being interlined between the forty third and forty fourth Lines of the second Page.

Attest William Jackson Secretary

done in Convention by the Unanimous Consent of the States present the Seventeenth Day of September in the Year of our Lord one thousand seven hundred and Eighty seven and of the Independance of the United States of America the Twelfth In witness whereof We have hereunto subscribed our Names,

G°. Washington
Presidt and deputy from Virginia

Delaware
Geo: Read
Gunning Bedford jun
John Dickinson
Richard Bassett
Jaco: Broom

Maryland
James McHenry
Dan of St Thos. Jenifer
Danl. Carroll

Virginia
John Blair
James Madison Jr.

North Carolina
Wm. Blount
Richd. Dobbs Spaight
Hu Williamson

South Carolina
J. Rutledge
Charles Cotesworth Pinckney
Charles Pinckney
Pierce Butler

Georgia
William Few
Abr Baldwin

New Hampshire
John Langdon
Nicholas Gilman

Massachusetts
Nathaniel Gorham
Rufus King

Connecticut
Wm. Saml. Johnson
Roger Sherman

New York
Alexander Hamilton

New Jersey
Wil: Livingston
David Brearley

72

Wm. Paterson
Jona: Dayton

Pennsylvania
B Franklin
Thomas Mifflin
Robt. Morris
Geo. Clymer
Thos. FitzSimons
Jared Ingersoll
James Wilson
Gouv Morris

APPENDIX E

The Bill of Rights

AMENDMENT I

Congress shall make no law respecting an establishment of religion, or prohibiting the free exercise thereof; or abridging the freedom of speech, or of the press; or the right of the people peaceably to assemble, and to petition the Government for a redress of grievances.

AMENDMENT II

A well regulated Militia, being necessary to the security of a free State, the right of the people to keep and bear Arms, shall not be infringed.

AMENDMENT III

No Soldier shall, in time of peace be quartered in any house, without the consent of the Owner, nor in time of war, but in a manner to be prescribed by law.

AMENDMENT IV

The right of the people to be secure in their persons, houses, papers, and effects, against unreasonable searches and seizures, shall not be violated, and no Warrants shall issue, but upon probable cause, supported by Oath or affirmation, and particularly describing the place to be searched, and the persons or things to be seized.

AMENDMENT V

No person shall be held to answer for a capital, or otherwise infamous crime, unless on a presentment or indictment of a Grand Jury, except in cases arising in the land or naval forces, or in the Militia, when in actual service in time of War or public danger; nor shall any person be subject for the same offence to be twice put in jeopardy of life or limb; nor shall be compelled in any criminal case to be a witness against himself, nor be deprived of life, liberty, or property, without due process of law; nor shall private property be taken for public use, without just compensation.

AMENDMENT VI

In all criminal prosecutions, the accused shall enjoy the right to a speedy and public trial, by an impartial jury of the State and district wherein the crime shall have been committed, which district shall have been previously ascertained by law, and to be informed of the nature and cause of the accusation; to be confronted with the witnesses against him; to have compulsory process for obtaining witnesses in his favor, and to have the Assistance of Counsel for his defence.

AMENDMENT VII

In suits at common law, where the value in controversy shall exceed twenty dollars, the right of trial by jury shall be preserved, and no fact tried by a jury, shall be otherwise reexamined in any Court of the United States, than according to the rules of the common law.

AMENDMENT VIII

Excessive bail shall not be required, nor excessive fines imposed, nor cruel and unusual punishments inflicted.

AMENDMENT IX

The enumeration in the Constitution, of certain rights, shall not be construed to deny or disparage others retained by the people.

AMENDMENT X

The powers not delegated to the United States by the Constitution, nor prohibited by it to the States, are reserved to the States respectively, or to the people.

AMENDMENT XI

Passed by Congress March 4, 1794. Ratified February 7, 1795.

Note: Article III, section 2, of the Constitution was modified by Amendment 11.

The Judicial power of the United States shall not be construed to extend to any suit in law or equity, commenced or prosecuted against one of the United States by Citizens of another State, or by Citizens or Subjects of any Foreign State.

AMENDMENT XII

Passed by Congress December 9, 1803. Ratified June 15, 1804.

Note: A portion of Article II, section 1 of the Constitution was superseded by the 12th Amendment.

The Electors shall meet in their respective states and vote by ballot for President and Vice-President, one of whom, at least, shall not be an inhabitant of the same state with themselves; they shall name in their ballots the person voted for as President, and in distinct ballots the person voted for as Vice-President, and they shall make distinct lists of all persons voted for as President, and of all persons voted for as Vice-President, and of the number of votes for each, which lists they shall sign and certify, and transmit sealed to the seat of the government of the United States, directed to the President of the Senate; — the President of the Senate shall, in the presence of the Senate and House of Representatives, open all the certificates and the votes shall then be counted; — The person having the greatest number of votes for President, shall be the President, if such number be a majority of the whole number of Electors appointed; and if no person have such majority, then from the persons having the highest numbers not exceeding three on the list of those voted for as President, the House of Representatives shall choose immediately, by ballot, the President. But in choosing the President, the votes shall be taken by states, the representation from each state having one vote; a quorum for this purpose shall consist of a member or members from two-thirds of the states, and a majority of all the states shall be necessary to a choice. [And if the House of Representatives shall not choose a President whenever the right of choice shall devolve upon them, before the fourth day of March next following, then the Vice-President shall act as President, as in case of the death or other constitutional disability of the President. --]* The person having the greatest number of votes as Vice-President, shall be the Vice-President, if such number be a majority of the whole number of Electors appointed, and if no person have a majority, then from the two highest numbers on the list, the Senate shall choose the Vice-President; a quorum for the purpose shall consist of two-thirds of the whole number of Senators, and a majority of the whole number shall be necessary to a choice. But no person constitutionally ineligible to the office of President shall be eligible to that of Vice-President of the United States.

Superseded by section 3 of the 20th Amendment.

AMENDMENT XIII

Passed by Congress January 31, 1865. Ratified December 6, 1865.

Note: A portion of Article IV, section 2, of the Constitution was superseded by the 13th Amendment.

Section 1.

Neither slavery nor involuntary servitude, except as a punishment for crime whereof the party shall have been duly convicted, shall exist within the United States, or any place subject to their jurisdiction.

Section 2.

Congress shall have power to enforce this article by appropriate legislation.

AMENDMENT XIV

Passed by Congress June 13, 1866. Ratified July 9, 1868.

Note: Article I, section 2, of the Constitution was modified by section 2 of the 14th Amendment.

Section 1.

All persons born or naturalized in the United States, and subject to the jurisdiction thereof, are citizens of the United States and of the State wherein they reside. No State shall make or enforce any law which shall abridge the privileges or immunities of citizens of the United States; nor shall any State deprive any person of life, liberty, or property, without due process of law; nor deny to any person within its jurisdiction the equal protection of the laws.

Section 2.

Representatives shall be apportioned among the several States according to their respective numbers, counting the whole number of persons in each State, excluding Indians not taxed. But when the right to vote at any election for the choice of electors for President and Vice-President of the United States, Representatives in Congress, the Executive and Judicial officers of a State, or the members of the Legislature thereof, is denied to any of the male inhabitants of such State, being twenty-one years of age,* and citizens of the United States, or in any way abridged, except for participation in rebellion, or other crime, the basis of representation therein shall be reduced in the proportion which the number of such male citizens shall bear to the whole number of male citizens twenty-one years of age in such State.

Section 3.

No person shall be a Senator or Representative in Congress, or elector of President and Vice-President, or hold any office, civil or military, under the United States, or under any State, who, having previously taken an oath, as a member of Congress, or as an officer of the United States, or as a member of any State legislature, or as an executive or judicial officer of any State, to support the Constitution of the United States, shall have engaged in insurrection or rebellion against the same, or given aid or comfort to the enemies thereof. But Congress may by a vote of two-thirds of each House, remove such disability.

Section 4.

The validity of the public debt of the United States, authorized by law, including debts incurred for payment of pensions and bounties for services in suppressing insurrection or rebellion, shall not be questioned. But neither the United States nor any State shall assume or pay any debt or obligation incurred in aid of insurrection or rebellion against the United States, or any claim for the loss or emancipation of any slave; but all such debts, obligations and claims shall be held illegal and void.

Section 5.

The Congress shall have the power to enforce, by appropriate legislation, the provisions of this article.

Changed by section 1 of the 26th Amendment.

AMENDMENT XV

Passed by Congress February 26, 1869. Ratified February 3, 1870.

Section 1.

The right of citizens of the United States to vote shall not be denied or abridged by the United States or by any State on account of race, color, or previous condition of servitude–

Section 2.

The Congress shall have the power to enforce this article by appropriate legislation.

AMENDMENT XVI

Passed by Congress July 2, 1909. Ratified February 3, 1913.

Note: Article I, section 9, of the Constitution was modified by Amendment 16.

The Congress shall have power to lay and collect taxes on incomes, from whatever source derived, without apportionment among the several States, and without regard to any census or enumeration.

AMENDMENT XVII

Passed by Congress May 13, 1912. Ratified April 8, 1913.

Note: Article I, section 3, of the Constitution was modified by the 17th Amendment.

The Senate of the United States shall be composed of two Senators from each State, elected by the people thereof, for six years; and each Senator shall have one vote. The electors in each State shall have the qualifications requisite for electors of the most numerous branch of the State legislatures.

When vacancies happen in the representation of any State in the Senate, the executive authority of such State shall issue writs of election to fill such vacancies: *Provided*, That the legislature of any State may empower the executive thereof to make temporary appointments until the people fill the vacancies by election as the legislature may direct.

This Amendment shall not be so construed as to affect the election or term of any Senator chosen before it becomes valid as part of the Constitution.

AMENDMENT XVIII

Passed by Congress December 18, 1917. Ratified January 16, 1919. Repealed by Amendment 21.

Section 1.

After one year from the ratification of this article the manufacture, sale, or transportation of intoxicating liquors within, the importation thereof into, or the exportation thereof from the United States and all territory subject to the jurisdiction thereof for beverage purposes is hereby prohibited.

Section 2.

The Congress and the several States shall have concurrent power to enforce this article by appropriate legislation.

Section 3.

This article shall be inoperative unless it shall have been ratified as an Amendment to the Constitution by the legislatures of the several States, as provided in the Constitution, within seven years from the date of the submission hereof to the States by the Congress.

AMENDMENT XIX

Passed by Congress June 4, 1919. Ratified August 18, 1920.

The right of citizens of the United States to vote shall not be denied or abridged by the United States or by any State on account of sex.

Congress shall have power to enforce this article by appropriate legislation.

AMENDMENT XX

Passed by Congress March 2, 1932. Ratified January 23, 1933.

Note: Article I, section 4, of the Constitution was modified by section 2 of this Amendment. In addition, a portion of the 12th Amendment was superseded by section 3.

Section 1.

The terms of the President and the Vice President shall end at noon on the 20th day of January, and the terms of Senators and Representatives at noon on the 3d day of January, of the years in which such terms would have ended if this article had not been ratified; and the terms of their successors shall then begin.

Section 2.

The Congress shall assemble at least once in every year, and such meeting shall begin at noon on the 3d day of January, unless they shall by law appoint a different day.

Section 3.

If, at the time fixed for the beginning of the term of the President, the President elect shall have died, the Vice President elect shall become President. If a President shall not have been chosen before the time fixed for the beginning of his term, or if the President elect shall have failed to qualify, then the Vice President elect shall act as President until a President shall have qualified; and the Congress may by law provide for the case wherein neither a President elect nor a Vice President shall have qualified, declaring who shall then act as President, or the manner in which one who is to act shall be selected, and such person shall act accordingly until a President or Vice President shall have qualified.

Section 4.

The Congress may by law provide for the case of the death of any of the persons from whom the House of Representatives may choose a President whenever the right of choice shall have devolved upon them, and for the case of the death of any of the persons from whom the Senate may choose a Vice President whenever the right of choice shall have devolved upon them.

Section 5.

Sections 1 and 2 shall take effect on the 15th day of October following the ratification of this article.

Section 6.

This article shall be inoperative unless it shall have been ratified as an Amendment to the Constitution by the legislatures of three-fourths of the several States within seven years from the date of its submission.

AMENDMENT XXI

Passed by Congress February 20, 1933. Ratified December 5, 1933.

Section 1.

The eighteenth article of Amendment to the Constitution of the United States is hereby repealed.

Section 2.

The transportation or importation into any State, Territory, or Possession of the United States for delivery or use therein of intoxicating liquors, in violation of the laws thereof, is hereby prohibited.

Section 3.

This article shall be inoperative unless it shall have been ratified as an Amendment to the Constitution by conventions in the several States, as provided in the Constitution, within seven years from the date of the submission hereof to the States by the Congress.

AMENDMENT XXII

Passed by Congress March 21, 1947. Ratified February 27, 1951.

Section 1.

No person shall be elected to the office of the President more than twice, and no person who has held the office of President, or acted as President, for more than two years of a term to which some other person was elected President shall be elected to the office of President more than once. But this Article shall not apply to any person holding the office of President when this Article was proposed by Congress, and shall not prevent any person who may be holding the office of President, or acting as President, during the term within which this Article becomes operative from holding the office of President or acting as President during the remainder of such term.

Section 2.

This article shall be inoperative unless it shall have been ratified as an Amendment to the Constitution by the legislatures of three-fourths of the several States within seven years from the date of its submission to the States by the Congress.

AMENDMENT XXIII

Passed by Congress June 16, 1960. Ratified March 29, 1961.

Section 1.

The District constituting the seat of Government of the United States shall appoint in such manner as Congress may direct:

A number of electors of President and Vice President equal to the whole number of Senators and Representatives in Congress to which the District would be entitled if it were a State, but in no event more than the least populous State; they shall be in addition to those appointed by the States, but they shall be considered, for the purposes of the election of President and Vice President, to be electors appointed by a State; and they shall meet in the District and perform such duties as provided by the twelfth article of Amendment.

Section 2.

The Congress shall have power to enforce this article by appropriate legislation.

AMENDMENT XXIV

Passed by Congress August 27, 1962. Ratified January 23, 1964.

Section 1.

The right of citizens of the United States to vote in any primary or other election for President or Vice President, for electors for President or Vice President, or for Senator or Representative in Congress, shall not be denied or abridged by the United States or any State by reason of failure to pay poll tax or other tax.

Section 2.

The Congress shall have power to enforce this article by appropriate legislation.

AMENDMENT XXV

Passed by Congress July 6, 1965. Ratified February 10, 1967.

Note: Article II, section 1, of the Constitution was affected by the 25th Amendment.

Section 1.

In case of the removal of the President from office or of his death or resignation, the Vice President shall become President.

Section 2.

Whenever there is a vacancy in the office of the Vice President, the President shall nominate a Vice President who shall take office upon confirmation by a majority vote of both Houses of Congress.

Section 3.

Whenever the President transmits to the President pro tempore of the Senate and the Speaker of the House of Representatives his written declaration that he is unable to discharge the powers and duties of his office, and until he transmits to them a written declaration to the contrary, such powers and duties shall be discharged by the Vice President as Acting President.

Section 4.

Whenever the Vice President and a majority of either the principal officers of the executive departments or of such other body as Congress may by law provide, transmit to the President pro tempore of the Senate and the Speaker of the House of Representatives their written declaration that the President is unable to discharge the powers and duties of his office, the Vice President shall immediately assume the powers and duties of the office as Acting President.

Thereafter, when the President transmits to the President pro tempore of the Senate and the Speaker of the House of Representatives his written declaration that no inability exists, he shall resume the powers and duties of his office unless the Vice President and a majority of either the principal officers of the executive department or of such other body as Congress may by law provide, transmit within four days to the President pro tempore of the Senate and the Speaker of the House of Representatives their written declaration that the President is unable to discharge the powers and duties of his office. Thereupon Congress shall decide the issue, assembling within forty-eight hours for that purpose if not in session. If the Congress, within twenty-one days after receipt of the latter written declaration, or, if Congress is not in session, within twenty-one days after Congress is required to assemble, determines by two-thirds vote of both Houses that the President is unable to discharge the powers and duties of his office, the Vice President shall continue to discharge the same as Acting President; otherwise, the President shall resume the powers and duties of his office.

AMENDMENT XXVI

Passed by Congress March 23, 1971. Ratified July 1, 1971.

Note: Amendment 14, section 2, of the Constitution was modified by section 1 of the 26th Amendment.

Section 1.

The right of citizens of the United States, who are eighteen years of age or older, to vote shall not be denied or abridged by the United States or by any State on account of age.

Section 2.

The Congress shall have power to enforce this article by appropriate legislation.

AMENDMENT XXVII

Originally proposed Sept. 25, 1789. Ratified May 7, 1992.

No law, varying the compensation for the services of the Senators and Representatives, shall take effect, until an election of representatives shall have intervened.

APPENDIX F

2004 Statistics of Lesbians and Gay Relationships verses
Heterosexual Relationships
Courtesy: Family Research Council
4/2/2004
http://www.frc.org/get.cfm?i=IS04C02

APPENDIX G
http://patdollard.com/2013/05/americans-must-read-4-stages-of-islamic-
conquest/

URGENT MUST-READ FOR ALL AMERICANS: The 4 Stages Of Islamic Conquest

May 27, 2013 39 Comments Jake Hammer

Excerpted from CIVILUS DEFENDUS

STAGE 1: INFILTRATION

Muslims begin moving to non-Muslim countries in increasing numbers and the beginning of cultural conflicts are visible, though often subtle.
o First migration wave to non-Muslim "host" country.
o Appeal for humanitarian tolerance from the host society.
o Attempts to portray Islam as a peaceful & Muslims as victims of misunderstanding and racism (even though Islam is not a 'race').
o High Muslim birth rate in host country increase Muslim population.
o Mosques used to spread Islam and dislike of host country & culture.
o Calls to criminalize "Islamophobia" as a hate crime.
o Threatened legal action for perceived discrimination.
o Offers of "interfaith dialogue" to indoctrinate non-Muslims.

How many nations are suffering from Islamic infiltration? One? A handful? Nearly every nation? The Islamic 'leadership" of the Muslim Brotherhood and others wish to dissolve each nation's sovereignty and replace it with the global imposition of Islamic sharia law. Sharia law, based on the koran, sira and hadith, condemns liberty and forbids equality and is inconsistent with the laws of all Western nations. As the author and historian Serge Trifkovic states:

"The refusal of the Western elite class to protect their nations from jihadist infiltration is the biggest betrayal in history."

STAGE 2: CONSOLIDATION OF POWER

Muslim immigrants and host country converts continue demands for accommodation in employment, education, social services, financing and courts.

o Proselytizing increases; Establishment and Recruitment of Jihadi cells.
o Efforts to convert alienated segments of the population to Islam.
o Revisionist efforts to Islamize history.
o Efforts to destroy historic evidence that reveal true Islamism.
o Increased anti-western propaganda and psychological warfare.
o Efforts to recruit allies who share similar goals (communists, anarchists).
o Attempts to indoctrinate children to Islamist viewpoint.
o Increased efforts to intimidate, silence and eliminate non-Muslims.
o Efforts to introduce blasphemy and hate laws in order to silence critics.
o Continued focus on enlarging Muslim population by increasing Muslim births and immigration.
o Use of charities to recruit supporters and fund jihad.
o Covert efforts to bring about the destruction of host society from within.
o Development of Muslim political base in non-Muslim host society.
o Islamic Financial networks fund political growth, acquisition of land.
o Highly visible assassination of critics aimed to intimidate opposition.
o Tolerance of non-Muslims diminishes.
o Greater demands to adopt strict Islamic conduct.
o Clandestine amassing of weapons and explosives in hidden locations.
o Overt disregard/rejection of non-Muslim society's legal system, culture.
o Efforts to undermine and destroy power base of non-Muslim religions including and especially Jews and Christians.

Is there a pattern here? Theo van Gogh is murdered in the Netherlands for 'insulting' Islam; the Organization of the Islamic Conference demands 'anti-blasphemy' laws through the United Nations; France is set afire regularly by 'youths' (read Muslims); the rise of (dis-) honor killings…holocaust denial…anti-Semitism…deception re the tenets of Islam; hatred toward Christians and Jews and Hindus and Buddhists. The pattern for all to see is the rise of Islamic intolerance and the covert/cultural jihad to remake host societies into sharia-compliant worlds – to remove host sovereignty and replace it with Islamic sharia law. Sharia law that condemns earthly liberty and individual freedom, that forbids equality among faiths and between the sexes, that rejects the concept of nations outside the global house of Islam, that of dar al-Islam.

STAGE 3: OPEN WAR w/ LEADERSHIP & CULTURE

Open violence to impose Sharia law and associated cultural restrictions; rejection of host government, subjugation of other religions and customs.
o Intentional efforts to undermine the host government & culture.
o Acts of barbarity to intimidate citizens and foster fear and submission.
o Open and covert efforts to cause economic collapse of the society.
o All opposition is challenged and either eradicated or silenced.
o Mass execution of non-Muslims.
o Widespread ethnic cleansing by Islamic militias.
o Rejection and defiance of host society secular laws or culture.
o Murder of "moderate" Muslim intellectuals who don't support Islamization.
o Destruction of churches, synagogues and other non-Muslim institutions.
o Women are restricted further in accordance with Sharia law.
o Large-scale destruction of population, assassinations, bombings.
o Toppling of government and usurpation of political power.
o Imposition of Sharia law

STAGE 4: Totalitarian ISLAMIC "THEOCRACY"

Islam becomes the only religious-political-judicial-cultural ideology.
o Sharia becomes the "law of the land.
o All non-Islamic human rights cancelled.
o Enslavement and genocide of non-Muslim population.
o Freedom of speech and the press eradicated.
o All religions other than Islam are forbidden and destroyed.
o Destruction of all evidence of non-Muslim culture, populations and symbols in country (Buddhas, houses of worship, art, etc).

The House of Islam ("peace"), dar al-Islam, includes those nations that have submitted to Islamic rule, to the soul crushing, liberty-condemning, discriminatory law of Sharia. The rest of the world in in the House of War, dar al-harb, because it does not submit to Sharia, and exists in a state of rebellion or war with the will of 'Allah.' No non-Muslim state or its citizens are "innocent," and remain viable targets of war for not believing in 'Allah.' The Christian, Jewish, Coptic, Hindu and Zoroastrian peoples of world have suffered under subjugation for centuries. The Dhimmi-esque are forbidden to construct houses of worship or repair existing ones, economically crippled by the heavy jizya (tax), socially humiliated, legally discriminated against, criminally targeted and generally kept in a permanent state of weakness, fear and vulnerability by Islamic governments.

It should be noted that forced conversions (Egypt) and slavery (Sudan) are still reported. Homosexuals have been hung in the public square in Iran. Young girls are married to old men. Apostates are threatened with death. "Honor" killings are routine. Women are legally second-class citizens, though Muslim males insist they are "treated better" than in the West. These more obvious manifestations may distract from some less obvious ones such as the lack of intellectual inquiry in science, narrow scope of writing, all but non-existent art and music, sexual use and abuse of youth and women, and the disregard for personal fulfillment, joy and wonder. Look into the eyes of a recently married 12 year old girl to see the consequence of the moral deprivation spawned by Islam.

The 4 Stages of Islamic Conquest is also available in pdf format for easy sharing as part of "Liberty vs Sharia"

APPENDIX H

"I Have a Dream"
Martin Luther King Jr.
October 16, 1965

Five score years ago, a great American, in whose symbolic shadow we stand today, signed the Emancipation Proclamation. This momentous decree came as a great beacon light of hope to millions of Negro slaves who had been seared in the flames of withering injustice. It came as a joyous daybreak to end the long night of their captivity.

But one hundred years later, the Negro still is not free. One hundred years later, the life of the Negro is still sadly crippled by the manacles of segregation and the chains of discrimination. One hundred years later, the Negro lives on a lonely island of poverty in the midst of a vast ocean of material prosperity. One hundred years later, the Negro is still languishing in the corners of American society and finds himself an exile in his own land. So we have come here today to dramatize a shameful condition.

In a sense we have come to our nation's capital to cash a check. When the architects of our republic wrote the magnificent words of the Constitution and the Declaration of Independence, they were signing a promissory note to which every American was to fall heir. This note was a promise that all men, yes, black men as well as white men, would be guaranteed the unalienable rights of life, liberty, and the pursuit of happiness.

It is obvious today that America has defaulted on this promissory note insofar as her citizens of color are concerned. Instead of honoring this sacred obligation, America has given the Negro people a bad check, a check which has come back marked "insufficient funds." But we refuse to believe that the bank of justice is bankrupt. We refuse to believe that there are insufficient funds in the great vaults of opportunity of this nation. So we have come to cash this check -- a check that will give us upon demand the riches of freedom and the security of justice. We have also come to this hallowed spot to remind America of the fierce urgency of now. This is no time to engage in the luxury of cooling off or to take the tranquilizing drug of gradualism. Now is the time to make real the promises of democracy. Now is the time to rise from the dark and desolate valley of segregation to the sunlit path of racial justice. Now is the time to lift our nation from the quick sands of racial injustice to the solid rock of brotherhood. Now is the time to make justice a reality for all of God's children.

It would be fatal for the nation to overlook the urgency of the moment. This sweltering summer of the Negro's legitimate discontent will not pass until there is an invigorating autumn of freedom and equality. Nineteen sixty-three is not an end, but a beginning. Those who hope that the Negro needed to blow off steam and will now be content will have a rude awakening if the nation returns to business as usual. There will be neither rest nor tranquility in America until the Negro is granted his citizenship rights. The whirlwinds of revolt will continue to shake the foundations of our nation until the bright day of justice emerges.

But there is something that I must say to my people who stand on the warm threshold which leads into the palace of justice. In the process of gaining our rightful place we must not be guilty of wrongful deeds. Let us not seek to satisfy our thirst for freedom by drinking from the cup of bitterness and hatred.

We must forever conduct our struggle on the high plane of dignity and discipline. We must not allow our creative protest to degenerate into physical violence. Again and again we must rise to the majestic heights of meeting physical force with soul force. The marvelous new militancy which has engulfed the Negro community must not lead us to a distrust of all white people, for many of our white brothers, as evidenced by their presence here today, have come to realize that their destiny is tied up with our destiny. They have come to realize that their freedom is inextricably bound to our freedom. We cannot walk alone.

As we walk, we must make the pledge that we shall always march ahead. We cannot turn back. There are those who are asking the devotees of civil rights, "When will you be satisfied?" We can never be satisfied as long as the Negro is the victim of the unspeakable horrors of police brutality. We can never be satisfied, as long as our bodies, heavy with the fatigue of travel, cannot gain lodging in the motels of the highways and the hotels of the cities. We cannot be satisfied as long as the Negro's basic mobility is from a smaller ghetto to a larger one. We can never be satisfied as long as our children are stripped of their selfhood and robbed of their dignity by signs stating "For Whites Only". We cannot be satisfied as long as a Negro in Mississippi cannot vote and a Negro in New York believes he has nothing for which to vote. No, no, we are not satisfied, and we will not be satisfied until justice rolls down like waters and righteousness like a mighty stream.

I am not unmindful that some of you have come here out of great trials and tribulations. Some of you have come fresh from narrow jail cells. Some of you have come from areas where your quest for freedom left you battered by the storms of persecution and staggered by the winds of police brutality. You have been the veterans of creative suffering. Continue to work with the faith that unearned suffering is redemptive.

Go back to Mississippi, go back to Alabama, go back to South Carolina, go back to Georgia, go back to Louisiana, go back to the slums and ghettos of our northern cities, knowing that somehow this situation can and will be changed. Let us not wallow in the valley of despair.

I say to you today, my friends, so even though we face the difficulties of today and tomorrow, I still have a dream. It is a dream deeply rooted in the American dream.

I have a dream that one day this nation will rise up and live out the true meaning of its creed: "We hold these truths to be self-evident: that all men are created equal."

I have a dream that one day on the red hills of Georgia the sons of former slaves and the sons of former slave owners will be able to sit down together at the table of brotherhood.

I have a dream that one day even the state of Mississippi, a state sweltering with the heat of injustice, sweltering with the heat of oppression, will be transformed into an oasis of freedom and justice.

I have a dream that my four little children will one day live in a nation where they will not be judged by the color of their skin but by the content of their character.

I have a dream today.

I have a dream that one day, down in Alabama, with its vicious racists, with its governor having his lips dripping with the words of interposition and nullification; one day right there in Alabama, little black boys and black girls will be able to join hands with little white boys and white girls as sisters and brothers.

I have a dream today.

I have a dream that one day every valley shall be exalted, every hill and mountain shall be made low, the rough places will be made plain, and the crooked places will be made straight, and the glory of the Lord shall be revealed, and all flesh shall see it together.

This is our hope. This is the faith that I go back to the South with. With this faith we will be able to hew out of the mountain of despair a stone of hope. With this faith we will be able to transform the jangling discords of our nation into a beautiful symphony of brotherhood. With this faith we will be able to work together, to pray together, to struggle together, to go to jail together, to stand up for freedom together, knowing that we will be free one day.

This will be the day when all of God's children will be able to sing with a new meaning, "My country, 'tis of thee, sweet land of liberty, of thee I sing. Land where my fathers died, land of the pilgrim's pride, from every mountainside, let freedom ring."

And if America is to be a great nation this must become true. So let freedom ring from the prodigious hilltops of New Hampshire. Let freedom ring from the mighty mountains of New York. Let freedom ring from the heightening Alleghenies of Pennsylvania!

Let freedom ring from the snowcapped Rockies of Colorado!

Let freedom ring from the curvaceous slopes of California!

But not only that; let freedom ring from Stone Mountain of Georgia!

Let freedom ring from Lookout Mountain of Tennessee!

Let freedom ring from every hill and molehill of Mississippi. From every mountainside, let freedom ring.

And when this happens, when we allow freedom to ring, when we let it ring from every village and every hamlet, from every state and every city, we will be able to speed up that day when all of God's children, black men and white men, Jews and Gentiles, Protestants and Catholics, will be able to join hands and sing in the words of the old Negro spiritual, "Free at last! free at last! thank God Almighty, we are free at last!"

www.ingramcontent.com/pod-product-compliance
Lightning Source LLC
Chambersburg PA
CBHW050417290526
45786CB00003B/1302